Instant
DVD Workshop 2

Mark Dileo

CMP**Books**

San Francisco, CA • New York, NY • Lawrence, KS

Published by CMP Books
an imprint of CMP Media LLC
600 Harrison Street, 6th Floor, San Francisco, CA 94107 USA
Tel: 415-947-6615; Fax: 415-947-6015

www.cmpbooks.com
email: books@cmp.com

Distributed in the U.S. by:
Publishers Group West
1700 Fourth Street
Berkeley, CA 94710
1-800-788-3123

Distributed in Canada by:
Jaguar Book Group
100 Armstrong Avenue
Georgetown, Ontario M6K 3E7 Canada
905-877-4483

For individual orders and for information on special discounts for quantity orders, please contact:

CMP Books Distribution Center, 6600 Silacci Way, Gilroy, CA 95020

email: cmp@rushorder.com; Web: www.cmpbooks.com

ISBN: 1-57820-243-4

Preface

The rate of computer and computer related advances never ceases to amaze me. Rewind five years to February of 1999. The fastest Intel processor was the PIII 500 while AMD's groundbreaking Athlon processor was 4 months from introduction. The fastest processors were barely able to playback MPEG-2 video without hardware assist, and DV camcorders were just beginning to catch the eye of consumers.

I had just begun to experiment with digital video editing and I posed a reflective question on a popular video editing forum, "When will consumers be able to edit MPEG-2 video on their computers using only software?" As usual, the answers ranged from the questionable "I'm doing it right now," to the outrageous "possibly never," to the more realistic consensus of "probably about 5 years." Needless to say, less than a year later we were editing MPEG-2 video on our home computers.

When I heard rumors of affordable DVD recorders hitting the streets a few years later, I knew the last link in the chain of affordable home video editing had appeared. Although users could record high quality digital video with DV camcorders, edit it and compress to MPEG-2 with little loss of quality, there was no easy way to view videos while preserving their high quality format. The loss in quality that occurred when copying digital video to VHS tape negated many of the advancements gained from using DV camcorders and nonlinear video editors in the first place.

In the same way that DV camcorders and nonlinear editors had before them, DVD burners, as they had come to be known, had trickled down from the domain of high-end commercial studios to become well within the financial reach of video enthusiasts and prosumers. And they brought along with them a new software category called DVD authoring.

DVD authoring is a unique blend of the technical, creating DVD discs that can play media in set-top DVD players, and the artistic, designing menus that are both intuitive to navigate and aesthetically pleasing. It is quite a thrill to be able to conceptualize and execute the production of a project from the shooting of video, to editing it, to designing the layout of the output medium. Welcome to the world of DVD authoring, the last link in the video production chain!

The author wishes to acknowledge the individuals who have contributed valuable suggestions to this work.

Mark Dileo

Technical Editor's Note

DVD Workshop 2.0 should really be called just DVD OH! for all the features it brings to the table. With the launch of DVD Workshop 1.0, Ulead brought the masses a tool that could bring more powerful DVD authoring tools to their knees. Features like hidden buttons, AC-3, motion menus, and so much more for under a thousand bucks, competing with tools that cost tens of thousands until recently, put Ulead permanently on the DVD authoring application map.

With the launch of DVD Workshop 2, Ulead has again leveled the playing field with multiple tracks of audio, subtitles, and other features previously found only on more expensive applications. This is a good thing, in my opinion, as it brings people closer to more easily and fluently expressing the messages that they've set out to express in one visual form or another.

In this book you will not find technical jargon that flies far over your head. In this book you will not find a need for deep mathematical skills. In this book you will not find pictures of Philo Farnsworth, one of the pioneers of video and television. What you will find are images of workflows, designed to answer the most common and basic questions relating to authoring DVDs. You'll find tips and tricks from an author and technical editor with real-world backgrounds in authoring DVDs and shooting video. You'll find tidbits of information that will improve your workflow by leaps and bounds, and magnificent revelations that will help you author Hollywood quality DVD menus. Of course, the quality of the video contained in these DVDs and menus is entirely left to the shooter and editors of the project.

Mark Dileo, a beta tester for the DVD Workshop product and a video editor of some repute in the New Jersey area, brings simple and comprehensive explanations of complex tasks, and provides tools and ideas for extremely high quality DVDs. Having a tool that can do the work simply isn't enough. Knowing how to use the tool is clearly the value in any situation. Many of us have hammers in our toolboxes, but how many of us know how to build a house? Dileo's explanations make it simple to build that house with the very powerful hammer Ulead has handed to its users.

Here at VASST, we pride ourselves on being user-oriented, seeking methods and techniques to present access to difficult tasks and objectives. Our live training tours, constant interface with various users of software and hardware tools, and our daily discussions with users in any number of forums and communities have helped us develop a method of delivering the information you need, in a cohesive and sensible manner. For more information on VASST, tutorials for your favorite audio and video tools, and for other training resources, please visit our website at http://www.vasst.com.

Thank you for reading our books,

Douglas Spotted Eagle
Technical Editor

Table of Contents

Introduction

The only permanent aspect in the world of computers is change. If a software application is released with a "1.0" after its name, version "2.0" is inevitable. Unfortunately, it has become commonplace for whole number version updates, i.e. 2 to 3, to not be deserving of the new version number as the new version often only includes fixes to the previous version and few, if any, really useful additional features.

Ulead's DVD Workshop 2.0 is an application that truly deserves it new moniker. While many users will find DVD Workshop 2.0 worthy of its "2.0" designation just for its new Subtitling Module, ability to use up to 8 Audio Tracks, CSS copy protection, Region Control, Motion Buttons, and Playlist control, I have come to admire some of the smaller improvements incorporated into DVD Workshop 2.0 since they enhance the creative process. No matter how technically "correct" a DVD menu may be, a great menu is not only functional, but also an artistic statement.

One of the less flamboyant improvements is the addition of real time previews for Motion Menus and Motion Buttons, which makes fiddling with these features a worthwhile endeavor since there is no waiting while DVD Workshop renders the preview. Now, you can apply a Motion Background and immediately see if it works with the Menu. Another huge timesaver is the ability to make Object boundaries visible, thus making it easy to spot and correct overlapping Objects. DVD Workshop 2.0 is a huge upgrade, encompassing a multitude of large and small improvements.

Although this book is aimed at the new user to DVD Workshop 2.0, the experienced user will also find a wealth of information contained in these pages, from technical information not found in the manual, to creative suggestions for authoring better projects. *Instant DVD Workshop* is written in a tutorial manner with an abundance of pictures guide the user through the DVD authoring process from capturing video to burning disks.

Here are some of the topics discussed in this book:

- The basics of installing DVD Workshop 2.0, creating a new project, and "how to" guides for capturing video using both analog and digital sources (Chapter 1)

- Editing media, from trimming video clips to creating slideshows (Chapter 2)

- How to create menus using either DVD Workshop 2.0's Menu Wizard or by building them from scratch (Chapter 3)

- The new advanced features of DVD Workshop

2.0, such as the Subtitling module that allows for the creating of up to 32 subtitle tracks for each Title in the project with language settings for each subtitle track. Advanced audio handling such as using up to 8 audio tracks with each Title, for narration, different languages, or background audio, just to name a few (Chapter 4).

- How to burn your project to a DVD and how to write your project to a digital linear tape drive in preparation for mass production. Using the digital linear tape option it is also possible to create dual layer (DVD-9) projects. DVD Workshop 2.0 also has the ability to apply CSS encryption, Macrovision®, and Region encoding to your finished project (Chapter 5)

- Project planning, editing for seamless menu to Title transitions, and how to effectively use a nonlinear editor to preprocess your video in "Make It Great" discussions. The tips in this chapter can help turn a good DVD project into a great one (Chapter 6)

Both new and experienced DVD Authors will find the step-by-step explanation of features make *Instant DVD Workshop* both a useful reference and learning tool. DVD Workshop 2.0 allows the user to express his or her creativity without itself getting in the way of that expression. *Instant DVD Workshop* will make sure that happens for you.

Chapter 1

Getting Started in DVD Workshop 2.0

In order to install Ulead's DVD Workshop 2.0 on your computer the operating system must be Windows XP or Windows 2000 with DirectX 9 or later. You can download DirectX from Microsoft's web site. You must also have 500MB of disk space available for program installation and a 16-bit color graphics card with a resolution of at least 1024x768.

For optimum application responsiveness, smooth previews, faster encoding, and faster disc creation times you should have a Pentium 4 2GHz processor, at least 512MB of RAM, and ample disk space for capturing and storing video and audio files, at least 40GB because one hour of digital video (DV) requires 13GB of hard disk space.

Because there isn't much use to creating (also called authoring) projects in DVD Workshop without a means to burn them to disc, you will need a recordable DVD drive to create DVDs or a CD-RW drive to create video CDs (VCDs and SVCDs).

If video from a Hi8 video camera or VCR is to be captured, then a video capture card that converts analog to DV or MPEG must be installed. The ADS DV Bridge is excellent for this because it is capable of converting to either DV or MPEG in real time. To capture video from a FireWire digital video camera you will need to have a FireWire port (often called IEEE 1394 or OHCI) on your computer. Make sure that any FireWire card you install has OHCI in the specifications.

Load Up!

Installing DVD Workshop

Insert the DVD Workshop disk into the CD or DVD drive. The Ulead setup screen will appear. Follow the directions to install the software. It is recommended to install the program into the default directory that setup automatically suggests.

If the Ulead setup screen does not appear:

Navigate to Windows Explorer>My Computer>CD/DVD drive and double-click the setup.exe program to initiate the installation routine.

If you purchased the downloadable version of DVD Workshop, double-click the setup.exe file you downloaded and follow the on-screen instructions.

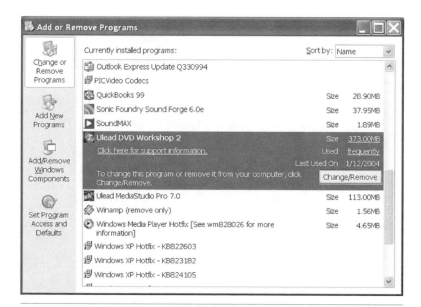

Uninstalling DVD Workshop

Navigate to: Control Panel>Add/Remove Programs and select DVD Workshop from the list of programs. Select Change/Remove, select Remove, and then select Next.

Follow the prompts to remove DVD Workshop. Notice that you may also repair a faulty DVD Workshop installation from this screen.

Overview of the Tools

The workflow, or steps required to create a DVD or VCD project, are broken down into five modules that are navigated by clicking tabs at the top of the workspace: Start, Capture, Edit, Menu, and Finish. These five tabs are always available.

The Start Tab—Creating a New Project

The Start screen is where a new project is created or an existing one is re-opened.

The Capture Tab—Recording Video

The Capture screen is where video is recorded to your hard drive for use in your project.

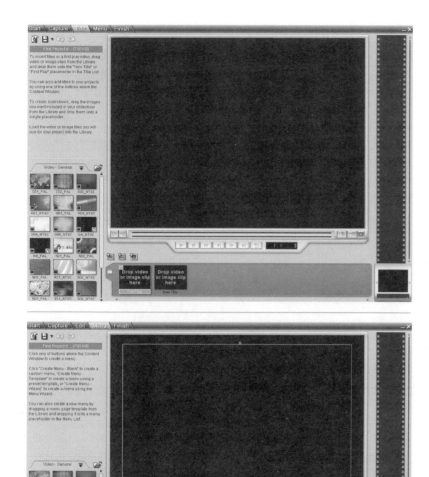

The Edit Tab—Adjusting Your Media

The Edit screen is where your media (audio and video files) are adjusted. Among other things, video clips can be trimmed, chapters can be added, the level of audio can be adjusted, additional audio tracks can be added, and subtitles can be added.

The Menu Tab—Laying Out the Project

The Menu screen is where menus are created with buttons that play clips. DVD Workshop provides many ways to customize your project with background audio, custom text, and a multitude of menu effects such as frames and shadows.

The Finish Tab – Previewing and Burning Your Project

The Finish screen is where the project may be previewed using a simulated remote control to make sure everything functions correctly before burning the project to disc. DVD Workshop allows for burning to disc, creating a disc image, creating a disc folder, or writing to digital linear tape (DLT), if you have the appropriate device connected to your computer.

In addition to the five screens or modules described above, there are three very important tools: the Library, the Title List, and the Chapter List.

The Library

The Library is where video clips, audio clips, still images, Ulead presets, and effects are stored for easy access while creating a project. The Library is displayed in the Capture, Edit, and Menu screens.

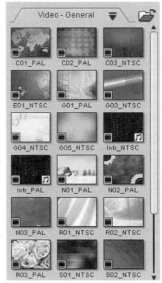

The Title List

The Title List is where media that will be played in the project is loaded. Each video clip or still image in the project must be placed into the Title List to be viewed in the final project. The Title List is displayed in the Capture, Edit, and Menu screens.

The Chapter List

Chapters are placeholders in videos that allow navigation to a specific point without having to fast-forward. When a chapter is added to a video clip, a thumbnail of the first frame of the chapter is added to the chapter list.

In the Beginning...

Before you can access any functions, a new project must be created.

How Do I Create a New Project?

To create a new project, click the New Project button. Notice that you can see the estimated size (97.5MB) of the opened project next to its name (First Project).

In the New Project dialog box, type a name for the project. Choose the final output media you will be using (DVD, VCD, or SVCD) and the TV system (NTSC for North America or PAL for Europe and Asia). The Subject and Description areas are used to record information about the project.

Where Does DVD Workshop Put My Project?

By default, DVD Workshop will create a folder with the same name as your project. For example, if your project is named First Project, then DVD Workshop will create a folder named First Project in the following location: My Documents>Ulead DVD Workshop>2.0>First Project. If you want to specify a different location, click the "..." button and browse to a new location for your project.

What Are Global Settings?

Select the Global Settings dialog box by left-clicking the hammer-and-wrench icon at the top left of the screen. Global settings are options that may affect the behavior of DVD Workshop throughout all the modules (screens).

Global Settings>Project Properties

Select Global Settings>Project Properties. Information about DVD Workshop and the current project settings are contained in this dialog box. You may also select the specification for video in the project, called the Disc Template Manager, by clicking the disc icon at the bottom right of this dialog.

Global Settings>Project Properties>Disc Template Manager

A disc template is a specification that DVD Workshop uses to render any video or audio if it is not compliant with the project settings (i.e. DVD). As an alternative, you may force DVD Workshop to render any audio or video file to the template. In general, you want to use the highest bitrate possible for your project that will fit on the target media (DVD, VCD, or SVCD) while not re-encoding any compliant media. This is definitely a balancing act!

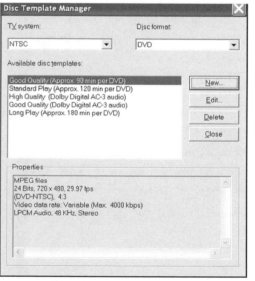

Global Settings>Project Properties>Disc Template Manager>New

Custom disc templates may be created from this dialog. Adjust the settings in the three tabs (Ulead DVD Workshop/ General/Compression) of this dialog to your preference. Fortunately, DVD Workshop allows you to select only attributes that are compliant with the media type selected when you created the project.

When you have that video clip that you can't get to stop flickering remember the General tab!

Global Settings>Project Properties>Disc Template Manager>Edit

New or existing disc templates may be edited in the same manner. For example, you may like all of the settings of a particular disc template except for the audio bitrate. To edit a disc template you would highlight the template to be edited, select Edit, select the Compression tab and change the audio bitrate setting.

Global Settings>Preferences

Insert tip:When you have that video clip that you can't get to stop flickering remember the General tab!

Select Global Settings>Preferences>General tab. Although the default settings of this dialog are good enough for most users, it's useful to be familiar with these settings if you want to work efficiently. The General tab provides a way to make changes to the number of undo operations, the linking behavior of files that have changed location, the flicker reduction control, and the "safety zone" setting for titling.

The Global Settings>Preferences>Default tab allows changes to the default duration of imported or captured images, the audio fade-in and fade-out duration for menus, and the default selection of menus and grids.

The Global Settings>Preferences>Capture tab enables an "OK" prompt before capture starts, automatic deinterlacing of still images, and options for captured image format and quality.

Global Settings>Relink

Select Global Settings>Relink. If a media file in the project is moved to a new location, selecting Relink will prompt you to locate the missing media file(s). If "Always show relink message" in Global Settings>Preferences>General is selected DVD Workshop will automatically prompt for media relinking information.

Global Settings>Disc Template Manager

Select Global Settings>Disc Template Manager. This is the same dialog described above that can also be accessed from the Project Preferences dialog.

Capture Concepts

How Do I Capture from My Analog Hi8 Camera or VCR?

To capture video you must either start a new project or open an existing project. After opening a project or creating a new one navigate to the Capture tab.

Connect the output video and audio jacks of your playback device such as a Hi8 camera or VCR to the input jacks of your capture card.

We'll work our way down the dialog boxes on the left of the Capture screen.

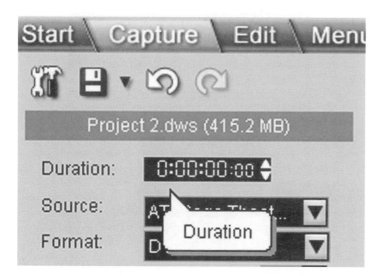

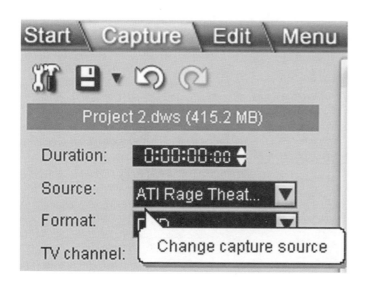

Can I Set the Capture Time?

You may also set the capture time by left-clicking in the Duration dialog and entering a time in the appropriate digit space. If you leave this dialog blank, capture will continue until manually stopped or disk space runs out.

What Device on My Computer Captures Analog Video?

The source dialog displays the analog device to which analog video is captured. This drop-down box (if you have more than one analog capture device installed) displays the capture cards available on the computer. If more than one capture card is installed, then select the one that you connected to the playback device.

Which Video Format Should I Select?

Select the appropriate project type for your project: DVD, VCD, or SVCD. DVD Workshop will select options that are compliant with the selected project. You may also select a particular media type: AVI, MPEG, or WMV. Other media that has been imported may need to be re-rendered upon the Finish step. If you have a TV tuner installed, then there will also be a channel selection dialog available below this dialog.

Where Does DVD Workshop Put My Captured Videos?

Select where capture video will be saved by clicking the folder icon next to the Capture Folder text. A second hard drive generally provides the best capture performance. Also remember to keep your hard drives defragmented for best capture results.

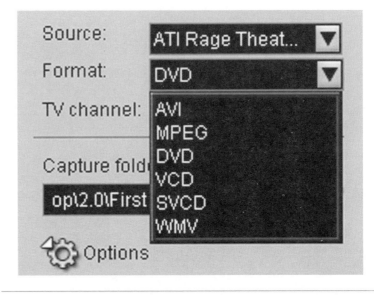

Do I Have to Worry About the Options Dialog?

You might not. If you play the video from your playback device and it previews on the monitor, then you might be ready to capture. The options available under this dialog vary depending on what video format you have selected and provide additional tweaking to the capture settings. Navigate to the DVD Workshop capture screen and select the Option button to view this dialog.

Device Control

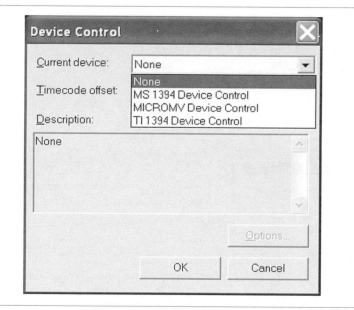

Select Edit>Options>Device Control to open the Device Control dialog. For analog capture "Current device" in this dialog should be set to None because analog playback devices can't be controlled through RCA or S-Video cables.

Change Capture Plug-in

Capturing MPEG without a hardware device that supports MPEG input may tax the processor to the point that frames are dropped. For best MPEG capture options, use a hardware device.

Select Options>Change Capture Plug-in. This dialog works with the Edit>Format dialog mentioned previously. If DVD was selected above, then the corresponding capture plug-in will be selected automatically in this dialog. Alternatively, you may select a capture plug-in from this dialog. If you're not sure, leave the default setting.

Video and Audio Capture Property Settings with DVD, VCD, SVCD, or MPEG Selected in the Format Dialog

Select Options>Video and Audio Capture Property Settings. Make sure the correct TV system, input source, and video format are selected. The DVD, VCD, and SCVD presets are excellent choices for quickly creating high-quality, project-compliant files. If you are experienced with MPEG you may want to use that format and tweak the settings. Also keep in mind that MPEG capture performance will depend on your system's speed.

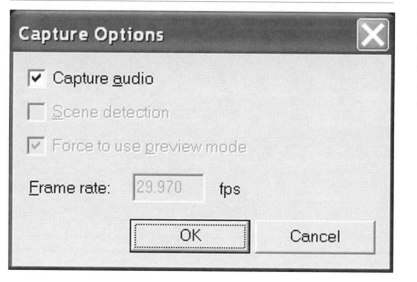

Advanced Video and Audio Capture Property Settings

Select Options>Video and Audio Capture Property Settings>Advanced. Most options in this dialog are grayed out if DVD, VCD, or SVCD is selected in Edit>Format because DVD Workshop selects the right choice for the format selected.

Capture Options (Available with DVD, VCD, SVCD, MPEG, or AVI Format Selected)

Select Option>Capture Options. Make sure the Capture Audio checkbox is checked if you want to capture audio with video. Scene detection is not available during analog capture, but you can select scenes later in the Edit screen.

Video and Audio Capture Property Settings with AVI Selected in Format Dialog

Select Option>Video and Audio Capture Property Settings. When capturing using AVI, it is best to use software compression, or the resulting file sizes will quickly fill up your hard drive, or result in many dropped frames during capture, or both.

Software Compression for AVI Format Video

Select Options>Video and Audio Capture Property Setting. Select the Software Compression checkbox and select the Advanced Box that becomes available. Select a compression type and quality and select OK.

Audio Format (Available Only with AVI Format Selected)

Select Options>Audio Format. If you select a template, then the format and attributes will be automatically selected. By selecting Untitled in the Name drop-down box you may choose your own format and attributes. The NTSC DVD standard for audio is PCM/48KHz (as shown) or AC3. AC3 cannot be selected from this dialog, so the audio will have to be encoded to AC3 during the Finish step by selecting this audio format in the disc template.

Video and Audio Capture Property Settings with WMV Selected in Format Dialog

Select Option>Video and Audio Capture Property Settings. WMV (Windows Media Video) is generally not used for DVD creation because it is a high-compression format and not yet compliant with set top DVD players. WMV files have to be re-rendered during the Finish step to create compliant DVDs. A WMV capture template can be chosen by choosing Select.

Profiles

Depending on the codecs installed in your system, a variety of WMV templates will be available from the Name drop-down menu.

Check for Playback

Start the capture playback device. If the above settings are correct, then you should see video playing in the preview screen. If not, check the previous settings, especially the input setting from Options>Video and Audio Capture Property Settings.

Setting the Capture Field Order (Available with All Formats Except WMV)

Start your playback device; video should start playing in the preview area. Select Options>Change Field Order. Select the correct field order for your capture device. If you aren't sure, select Detect in the Change Field Order dialog box, and DVD Workshop will determine the field order of the source video and select the correct option. Click OK when finished.

Profiles

Name:

Windows Media Video 8 for Broadband (NTSC, 1400 Kbps) ▼

Description:

Video:
Frame Size (W x H) = 320 x 240 (pixels), 24 bits/pixel

Audio:
PCM, 44100 Hz (samples/sec), 16 bits/sample, Stereo

| OK | Cancel | Help |

Change Field Order

Field order: Upper Field First ▼

Processing... 80 %

| Detect | OK | Cancel |

Starting and Stopping Capture

Click the Capture Video icon to begin capture. Capture will begin, and the Capture Video icon will turn into an icon labeled Stop Capture. Click this button again to stop capture.

What Does the Add Video to Title List Checkbox Do?

If the Add Video to Title List checkbox is selected, then after captured is stopped the captured clip will be added to the Title List displayed at the bottom of the screen. The Title List contains the media to be played in your project. You may delete a clip from the Title List area by selecting it and selecting the delete key. You can change the order of clips by left-clicking the clip and dragging it to a new location.

Are Captured Video Clips Added to the Library?

All captured video clips are automatically added to the Video – General Library folder located at the lower-left portion of the screen.

How Do I Capture Digital Video from My FireWire-Equipped Digital Camcorder?

To capture video you must either start a new project or open an existing project. Then navigate to the Capture tab.

Connect the camcorder to your computer using the FireWire connection and turn the camcorder onto the VCR setting. The Ulead Capture Manager dialog box will appear on your screen indicating that it has found a new device. Click Yes.

If this dialog box does not appear after 20 seconds or so, turn off the camcorder and turn it on again, making sure to set it to VCR and not Camera.

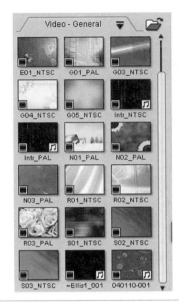

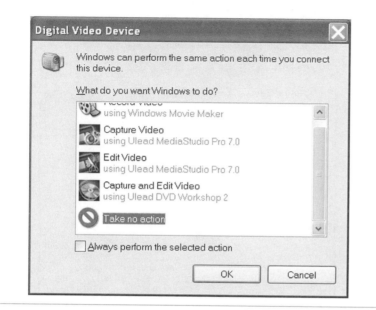

Next the Windows Digital Video Device dialog may appear. If it does, select the "Take no action" option. You might also want to check the "Always take this option" box to avoid this message in the future.

After a few moments Windows will detect your new hardware, and the first frame of the video will be displayed on the preview screen. The source dialog generally will display the brand of your camcorder and the type of device control.

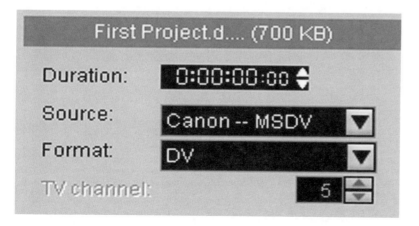

DVD Workshop Won't Control My DV Camcorder.

Select Options>Select Device Control. Generally, MS 1394 device control works for most DV camcorders. If it doesn't work, select another option.

Additional device control options are found by selecting Options from the Device Control dialog. The default selections are generally adequate.

Device Control

Current device: MS 1394 Device Control

None
MS 1394 Device Control
MICROMV Device Control
TI 1394 Device Control

Timecode offset:

Description:

Supports DV camcorder

Options...

OK   Cancel

MS Device Control Options

Active device: CANON

Pre-roll time: 300 ms

Transmit pause time: 2500 ms

Record pause time: 2500 ms

Delay record time: 300 ms

OK   Cancel

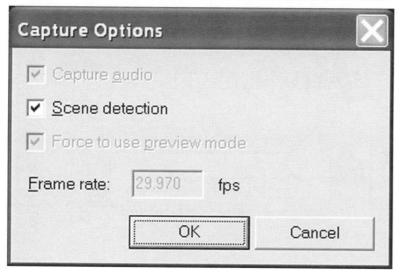

What Video Formats Can I Capture Using the FireWire Connection to My DV Camcorder?

Depending on the drivers installed in your system, you may be able to capture video in a few different formats. Select Options>Change Capture Plug-in to select a capture plug-in. The default DV capture plug-in is the Ulead Direct-Show Capture Plug-in. This option will capture DV video from your camera without re-encoding the video. At the Finish step the video will be converted to the project template. You may also encode the DV video to MPEG-2 while capturing in real time by selecting the Ulead DSW MPEG Capture Plug-in. See the MPEG vs. FireWire Capture section at the end of this chapter for more information.

How Do I Use Scene Detection While Capturing?

Select Options>Capture Options... If you check the "Scene detection" box, a separate video clip will be created for each scene change in the video. Leave this unselected if you want one long (contiguous) capture video.

Which Type of DV Should I Select?

Without getting too technical, DV type-1 interleaves the video and audio data together, but DV type-2 keeps the video and audio data separate. It is recommended to select DV type-1 if available to avoid possible audio or video sync issues. Select Options>DV Type to change this option.

From this point, capture is initiated in the same manner as with analog capture described in the previous section. Position your camcorder to the location you wish to capture and click the Capture Video icon. Click this button again to stop capture.

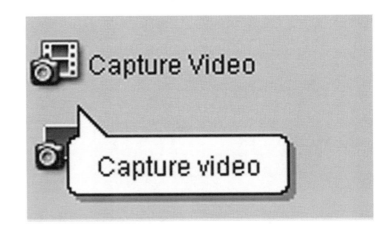

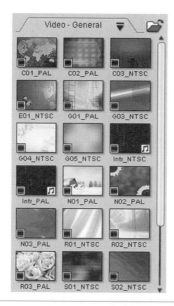

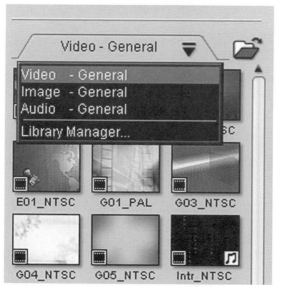

The Library

The Library is where all media such as video clips, audio clips, still images, graphics, menu templates, text effects and other predefined objects are located for easy access. The Library is visible from the Capture, Edit, and Menu screens, but some of the folder options appear only from certain modes in DVD Workshop. The images in the Library are called thumbnails.

Working with Video Clips in the Library

Select the Video – General folder in the library by left-clicking the down arrow next to the library and selecting Video – General if it is not already selected.

Management, Management, Management!

Management of media assets is critical to efficient authoring. As you become more experienced at authoring high-quality DVDs, this quickly becomes apparent. Get in the habit of managing media with these tools early on, and you'll be much more proficient at authoring.

Right-clicking on a video clip brings up a dialog box with various options. Selecting edit will automatically select the Edit screen and load the selected clip into the preview window.

How to Delete a Video Clip from the Library

There are two ways to delete a video clip from the Library:

• Left-click the clip and press the Delete key

• Right-click the clip and select Delete from the pop-up menu

After selecting Delete, DVD Workshop will ask if you want to delete the thumbnail. Click Yes if you want to delete the thumbnail.

DVD Workshop will then ask you if you want to delete the file from your hard drive. Select the appropriate response. "No to all" and "Yes to all" are included in the event more than one file was initially selected.

If you select Yes, files contained in the Library will not only be deleted from the project but also from your hard drive. Be sure you want to delete these files before selecting Yes.

Ulead DVD Workshop ✕

⚠ Do you want to delete the thumbnail?

[13031:1:402]   [**Yes**]   [**No**]

Ulead DVD Workshop ✕

Do you want to delete the file ?

C:\Documents and Settings\Mark\My Documents\Ul...\040113-002.AVI

[Yes] [Yes to All] [No] [No to All] [Cancel]

How Do I Select Multiple Thumbnails in the Library?

Hold the Control key while left-clicking the mouse to select multiple thumbnails one at a time. Hold the Shift key while left-clicking the mouse to select a group of thumbnails. In the screenshot all but the last three thumbnails are selected.

Can I Customize the Library?

Yes, in addition to the Video – General, Image – General, and Audio – General default folders in the Library it is possible to create a custom folder in the Library. Select the Library Manager from the drop-down menu in the Library.

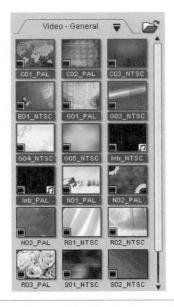

Click New in the Library Manager dialog box.

Type the name in the New Custom Folder dialog box, add a description of the folder if you like, and click OK. A custom Library folder may also be edited and deleted from the Library Manager dialog.

The Library Manager can also be accessed by selecting Global Settings>Library Manager.

Video Playback in DVD Workshop

How Do I Load a Video Clip into the Preview Window in the Edit Screen?

Video clips are viewed in the Edit tab. There are three ways to load a clip.

- Double-click a clip in the Title list or Library.
- Right-click a clip in the Title List or Library and select Edit.
- Drag and drop the clip from the Title List or Library to the Preview Window.

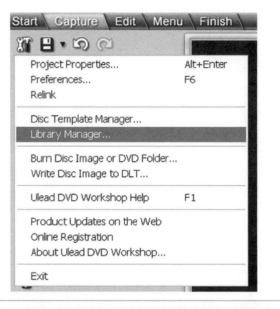

Play [Enter]
Hold SHIFT key to play selected area only [Space]

Playing Back a Video Clip

To play back the video clip, click the right-arrow icon in the playback controls. Pressing the Enter key will also start playback. Pressing the spacebar will alternately pause and restart playback. There are also controls to move forward or back one frame (or I-frame) at a time, move forward or back to the next edit point, and a repeat play button.

Always edit on I-frames to avoid problems between frames.

Using the Jog Bar to Move Around a Video Clip

By left-clicking and dragging the Jog Bar above the player controls you can quickly move around a video clip to locate important scenes.

Jog Bar. Press [Ctrl] while dragging the Jog Bar to change the chapter's current position.

Can the Time Counter Be Used to Move the Jog Bar to a Specific Time-code?

Specific timecode can also be input into the counter to move the Jog Bar directly to a certain location in the video clip. For example, to move to 15 seconds in the current video clip, left-click the seconds portion of the counter once. It will begin blinking. Enter "15." The Jog Bar will move to 0:00:15:00, and the corresponding video will show in the preview window.

Go to a specific timecode

Importing Video Clips

Video clips can be loaded into the Library or directly into the Title List. We'll learn about the former option in the next chapter. DVD Workshop can also directly import video from unencrypted DVDs.

Importing Video Clips into the Library

Make sure that the Video – General folder is selected in the Library drop-down menu.

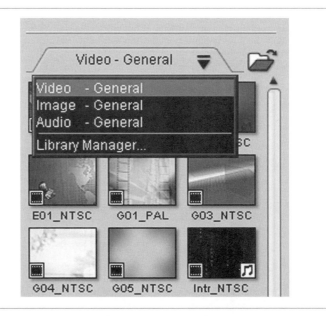

Select the Load Video File icon just to the right of the Library.

Browse to the location of the file to be loaded, select it, and click Open. The selected video clip will be added to the Video – General folder of the Library.

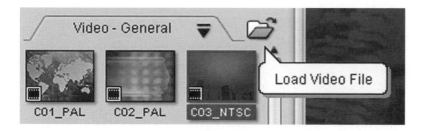

Also, you can right-click anywhere in the Library and select Load File to open the Load Video dialog.

Can I Import Video from a DVD?

Yes, but the DVD video must be unencrypted and the video must be imported directly into the Title List. Navigate to the Edit tab. Select the Import from DVD icon just above and to the left of the Title List.

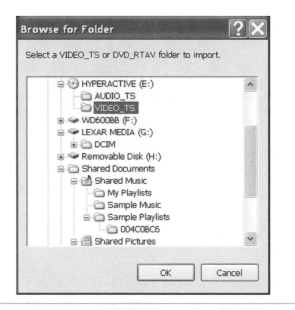

Browse to the VIDEO_TS folder, select it and click OK. The OK button will not be available until DVD Workshop detects compatible media.

From the Select Scenes to Capture dialog box, highlight the scene or scenes to be captured. Click OK. The scenes will begin to be captured to the Title List and to the hard drive to the directory where the currently opened project is located.

Ripping media from copyrighted DVD's or VHS tapes is a violation of copyright law. Making a DVD from a VHS tape for your own personal use is legal, if you destroy the VHS tape after copying to DVD.

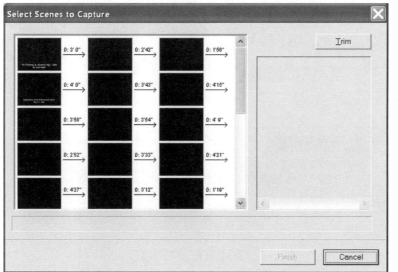

Trimming DVD Video Clips Before Loading into the Title List

Use a captured image as a background for a DVD menu, as a button, or as an image layered on a menu as a composite.

Select Edit>Import from DVD, browse to the VIDEO_TS folder, and click OK. Select trim and move the "mark in, mark out" points to the desired video beginning and end locations. All of the video contained in the VIDEO_TS folder will be available in the preview window. You may trim out and import many different clips by repeating this procedure. Remember that you may import DVD video either from DVD disc or from your hard drive.

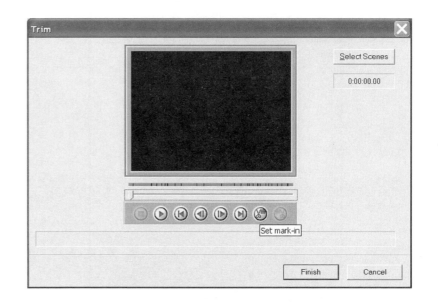

Capturing Still Images

How Do I Capture Still Images?

Connect either a DV camcorder or an analog playback device to your computer. From the Capture tab set up DVD Workshop as specified in the section above. Capturing stills is much the same as capturing video. The video is played back, and the Edit>Capture Image icon is selected at the appropriate moment. The captured image will be added to the Image folder in the Library.

How Do I Change the Format That Still Images Are Captured In?

Still images may be captured in a loss-less bitmap format or the JPEG format, which has different levels of quality. Select Global Settings>Preferences> Capture tab to adjust these settings. Because video is in a relatively low resolution compared to photographic images, it is best to capture screen shots in the lossless BMP format.

Importing Still Images

Still images may be imported by load-ing them into the Library.

Adding Images to the Library

Make sure that the Image – General folder is selected in the Library drop-down menu.

Left-click the folder icon to the right of the Library.

From the Load Image File dialog box, select the image you would like to load and click OK. The selected image file will be loaded into the Image – General folder of the Library.

You may also right-click anywhere in the Library and select Load File.

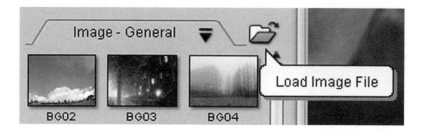

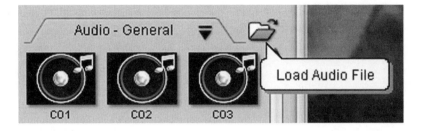

Library Importing Logic

You may have noticed that the Load Media Folder icon to the right of the Library will import whatever type of media is currently selected in the Library drop-down menu. For example, if the Library is showing the Audio – General folder, then this icon will load audio files into the library. The balloon text that appears when the mouse cursor is placed over the folder icon will read Load Audio File.

Saving and Reopening a Project

Saving a Project

A project can be saved from any tab except the Finish tab by clicking the floppy disc icon at the top-left area of the screen.

After clicking the floppy disc icon, a dialog box will appear that will inform you of the progress of the save.

Projects may also be saved by selecting Save from the option in the drop-down menu that appears when selecting the down arrow next to the floppy disc icon.

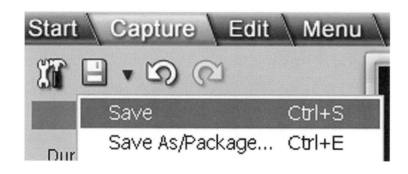

Backing Up Project Files

The project can be backed up to another location by selecting Save As from the drop-down menu, typing in a project name, and selecting a location. Only the project files will be stored in this new location, not the media that is used in the project.

Is There a Way to Backup an Entire Project, Media and All?

Yes, it is possible to save the project files and all of the media that was used in the project by ticking the "Package all files" checkbox in the Save As dialog. Packaging provides a convenient means to back up an entire project to one location for archiving if you later want to modify the project. If you package a project with large media files, it may take a while.

Opening a Project

DVD Workshop will keep a few of the recently used projects handy for fast access by displaying them by name as hyperlinked text. Opening a project in the recently used list is as easy as left-clicking the project title.

If the project you wish to open is not in the Recent Projects list, click the Open Project icon and browse to the location of the project file. If you can't find your project, remember to search for files with the extension .dws.

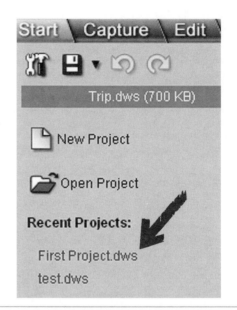

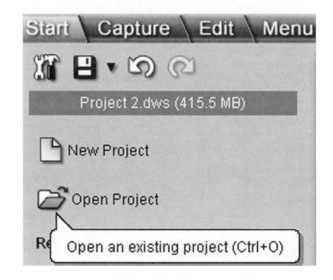

MPEG vs. FireWire Capture

The final format for all video files in a DVD, VCD, or SVCD project is MPEG, so all video files will either have to be captured in a project compliant with the MPEG format or be converted to one in the Finish step.

The quality of MPEG video captured in real time will not be as high as DV FireWire captured video encoded to MPEG in the Finish step. This is because there are no constraints for the computer to keep up with the video coming from the camcorder.

By the same reasoning, you may achieve better-quality video by recording analog sources (Hi8 or VCR) to a low-compression AVI format such as MJPEG and then encoding to MPEG at the Finish step rather than recording directly to the MPEG format during capture. Another benefit of this workflow is that DVD Workshop will be more responsive while editing non-MPEG video clips.

Video Compression

Compression:

No Recompression

DV Video Encoder
Indeo® video 5.10 Compression Filter
MJPEG Compressor
PICVideo MJPEG Compressor
Cinepak Codec by Radius
Intel 4:2:0 Video V2.50

About...

Configure...

Cancel

OK

Chapter 2

Editing Video in DVD Workshop 2.0

The Edit screen is where all of the media is trimmed and adjusted in preparation for use in your DVD project.

Because DVD Workshop is a professional application, understanding some technical information will help you get the most out of the software.

The Edit step of DVD Workshop 2.0 is where titles may be manipulated so that they are more appealing to the DVD viewer. Titles may be trimmed so that unnecessary video is deleted, up to 8 audio tracks may be added to each title in the project, and chapter points may be added to each title so that the viewer can quickly skip from scene to scene. In addition, you may easily create slideshows with background audio in the Edit step.

The Edit Screen

Add Audio Tracks

Add Chapters

Trim Clips

Create Slideshows

What Are I-Frames?

Video used in DVDs is compressed to the MPEG-2 format. MPEG-2 can produce high-quality video while taking up very little disk space because only some frames of the video contain all of the data required to produce a frame. These frames are called I-frames, for "intraframes."

How Are the Other MPEG-2 Video Frames Generated?

The other frames in a MPEG video are called P-frames or predictive frames, and B-frames or bidirectional frames. P-frames use data from the previous frame to generate a frame, and B-frames use data from both of the frames on either side of it to generate an image.

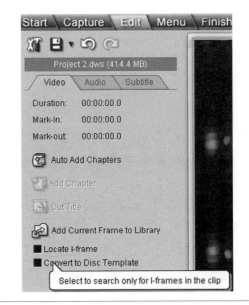

Why Are I-Frames Important for DVD Authoring?

While editing MPEG video clips, you should use I-frames. Because I frames contain all of the frame data, it is much easier for DVD Workshop to lock onto an I-frame for editing. Using frames other than I-frames could result in having black video frames in your project.

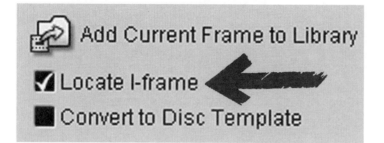

What is a GOP?

A GOP is a "group of pictures," or a group of I-, B-, and P-frames. These frames may be arranged in different orders to achieve the best video-quality-to-bitrate ratio for a specific video clip. One of the reasons commercial DVDs look so good (besides the great source video), is because compressionists tweak the MPEG settings to the nth degree!

I = Intra video picture
B = Bidirectional picture
P = Predictive picture

Variable Bit Rate (VBR) vs. Constant Bit Rate (CBR) Encoding

MPEG video encoded with constant bitrate allocates the same number of bits to every GOP, while variable-bit-rate-encoded video varies the amount of data allocated to each GOP of frames to maximize quality-to-bitrate ratio. Navigate to Global Settings>Disc Template Manager>Edit to select VBR.

Check Your MPEG-2-Encoded Video on a TV

Video encoded to MPEG-2 sometimes looks darker than the original video. It's a good plan to render your video and check it on a TV so that you can make adjustments before burning your project to DVD. If your settop DVD player will play DVD-RW discs, you may want to create a test disc.

Viewing the Properties of a Video Clip

You can view the video properties of any video clip (or image) by right-clicking on the video thumbnail and selecting Properties.

Ready? Set? Go!

It's a good idea to plan your DVD project by sketching it on paper.

Where Do I Start?

The figure on the right shows a simple project that begins with a first-play video, includes three video buttons on the main menu, and a scene-selection menu for each of these videos.

Gather Your Assets

Assemble your media into the Library. This media may include captured video and images, imported video and images, and audio files. The creative process will flow better if you don't have to constantly stop to track down your media.

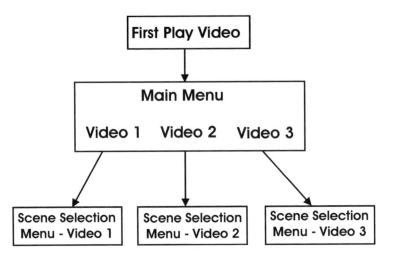

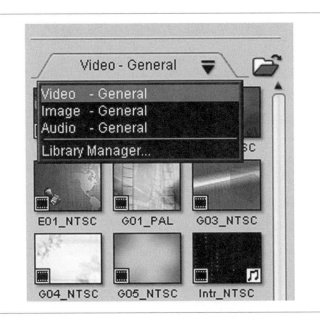

Keeping Your Assets Organized

It is not unusual while working on a project to grab a video clip here, an image there, and before you know it your assets are coming from all over your computer system! It's good practice when possible to first move all of the media to be used in your project into one folder. In this example the folder named Media was created in the project directory.

Create a new folder for your media by Navigating to Windows Explorer>File>New Folder.

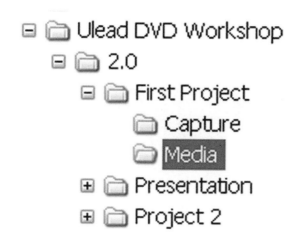

Determining Titles and Chapters

After deciding what video clips will be included in your project, you must decide what points within the clips the viewer will be able to access directly.

What Is a Title?

A title is another way to refer to a video clip or image. Video clips or images that are added to the Title List are called titles.

The icon in the bottom left of the title thumbnail indicates whether it is a video clip or an image clip. The icon in the bottom right indicates whether there is sound associated with a video clip.

The first title is a video clip with sound. The second title is a video clip without sound. The third title is an image.

What Is a Chapter?

A chapter is a playback point created within a title (video clip). For example, if you set playback points at two minutes and five minutes in a nine-minute title, then there would be three chapters in this title. The first chapter would be two minutes long (2-0), the second chapter three minutes long (5-2), and the third chapter four minutes long (9-5). The screenshot on the left shows the Chapter List with three chapters.

The Title Selector

Using the Title Selector, you can quickly move from one title to the next to view and edit the chapters located in the title. Click the right-arrow icon if you want to move to the next title.

Assembling a Title List

Adding media to the Title List is the first step to building a project. The Title List is visible from the Capture, Edit, and Menu screens.

How Do I Add Video Clips to the Title List?

There are multiple ways to add video clips to the Title List. One way is to right-click a video clip in the Library and select Add to Title List from the pop-up menu.

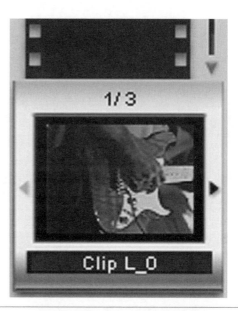

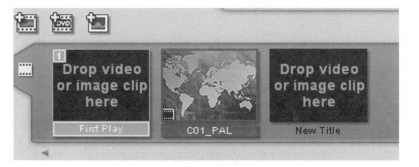

The video clip C01_PAL has been added to the Title List.

You can also left-click on a video clip and drag the clip into the Title List. The vertical line between the First Play and New Title placeholder in the screenshot below indicates that a video is about to be dropped into the Title List.

Video clips can also be imported directly to the Title List by selecting the Add Video icon above the Title List in the Edit screen.

Browse to the location of the file to be loaded, select it and click Open.

Adding Still Images to the Title List

Still images may be added to the Title List in the same manner as described for video clips above. You can right-click an image in the Library and select Add to Title List.

Images may also be dragged to from the Library to the Title List.

Images can be imported directly to the Title List by clicking the Add Image icon above the Title List from the Edit screen.

Changing the Order of Titles in the Title List

The order of titles in the Title List can be changed by dragging the title to another location by holding right-clicking on the title and moving it to a new location in the Title List.

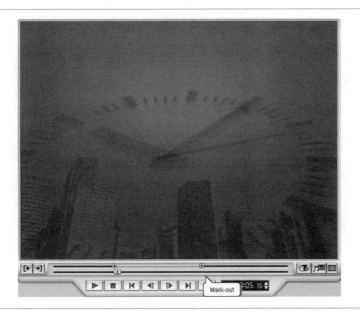

Using the same procedure described above, thumbnails in the Library can also be rearranged.

Trimming Video and Audio Clips

If possible, trim video and audio clips in a nonlinear editor. Project-compliant clips will be re-encoded if trimmed in DVD Workshop, with some reduction in video quality. Although the following tutorial uses video clips, the procedure to trim audio clips is identical.

What Does It Mean to Trim a Video Clip?

Trimming a video clip means adjusting the clip so that only part of it plays. This is part of the editing process. Some of the beginning of the clip could be trimmed, some of the end, or both the beginning and the end. Video clips in the Library or the Title List may be trimmed in the Edit screen.

What Are Mark-In/Mark-Out Points?

A mark-in point is a setting that designates where the video in the clip should begin playing. For example, if the mark-in point is set at 10 seconds, then the trimmed clip will begin to play 10 seconds into the video clip. A mark-out point is where the video is designated to end playing.

Trimming a Clip

Load a video clip from the Library or Title List into the Preview window by right-clicking the video clip and selecting Edit from the pop-up menu or by double-clicking the clip.

Click the Locate I-frame checkbox to avoid corrupt frames in the project. Note that you will not be able to access all frames of the title, only the I-frames.

Move slider on the Jog Bar to the location where you would like the video to begin playing.

Add Current Frame to Library

☑ Locate I-frame

■ Convert to Disc Template

Jog Bar. Press [Ctrl] while dragging the Jog Bar to change the chapter's current position.

Select the mark-in icon to set the
mark-in point.

The lack of shading before the mark-in
location in the Trim Bar indicates the
new start location of the title.

Move the slider in the Jog Bar to the location where you would like the video to stop playing.

Select the mark-out icon to set the mark-out point.

Jog Bar. Press [Ctrl] while dragging the Jog Bar to change the chapter's current position.

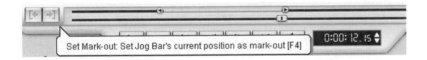

Set Mark-out: Set Jog Bar's current position as mark-out [F 4]

Using the Time Counter to Set Mark-In and Mark Out Points

Remember that the slider in the Jog Bar may also be moved to a specific position by typing a time into the counter.

Viewing Trimmed Title Information

The duration of the trimmed title and the location of the mark-in and mark-out points can be viewed in the Options Panel located near the top-left part of the Edit screen.

Trimming a Title by Dragging the Trim Bar

You may also trim the clip by dragging the mark-out and mark-in sliders on the Trim Bar (just above the Jog Bar) to the desired locations.

How Do I Playback Only the Trimmed Portion of a Video Clip?

Pressing the spacebar will play the trimmed portion of the clip, and clicking the Play icon or pressing the Enter key will play back the entire clip. If you want to continue playing back the trimmed portion of the clip, then select the Repeat icon and press the Spacebar.

Splitting Clips

As with trimming clips, when possible, splitting clips should be performed in a non-linear editor to avoid re-rendering compliant video.

Splitting a Video Clip from the Title List

Load a video clip into the Preview Window by right-clicking the thumbnail and selecting Edit from the pop-up menu, or by double-clicking the thumbnail.

Move the slider in the Jog Bar to where you would like to make the cut.

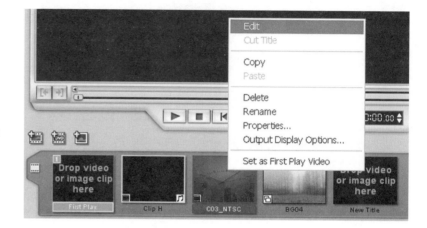

Click the Cut Title icon to split the title into two separate titles.

The second half of the clip will remain in the Preview window, and the mark-in and mark-out points will reflect the new duration of the clip. Note that the video clip was not actually cut into two segments; a copy was created with new mark-in and mark-out points.

Two video clips (titles) will now be located in the Title List. The first one will have the original name and contain the video for the first half of the clip. The second clip will have a number designation added to its name, "_0" in this example.

Splitting a Video Clip from the Library

Video clips in the Library may be split in the same manner as titles in the Title List. The split clips will be placed in the Library folder where the original clip was located. In this example Clip SV was split into Clip SV and Clip SV_0

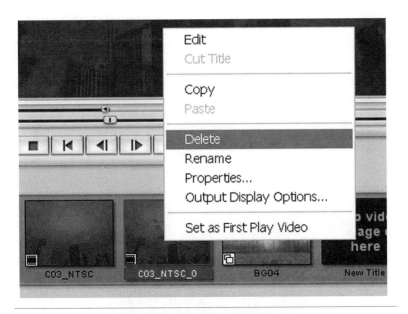

How Do I Restore a Split Video Clip?

A trimmed video clip can be restored to its original state by deleting either section of the split clip and moving the mark-in and mark-out points to the beginning and end of the video clip.

Splitting Video Clips by Scenes

Can I Split a Video Clip into Scenes After It Has Been Captured?

Absolutely! Right-click on a video clip in the Library and select Split by Scene

Select Scan in the Scenes dialog.

DVD Workshop will scan the selected clip and split it into smaller clips by scene detected. All clips with check-boxes checked will be automatically loaded into the Library when you click OK.

Scene Detection Sensitivity

Select Scene Detection>Options. You can increase or decrease the sensitivity that DVD Workshop uses to detect scenes. For example, if scenes are not being detected that you would like to be detected, increase the sensitivity.

Can I Rejoin Scenes That Scene Detection Created?

DVD Workshop can join consecutive scenes, or put video clips back together. Select the lower scene of the two scenes in the menu you want joined and click Join. Notice that the first two clips have 47 and 33 frames.

Be sure your DV camera has the date and time set, or no scenes will be created on your videotape, and only light and luma changes will be used to detect scene changes.

The two scenes will be joined into one, with a "+1" in the "Joined" column, indicating that this scene is joined with the scene that was following it. Notice that the joined video clip has 80 frames, or the combined total of the two joined clips (47+33=80).

Renaming a Title

You may rename a title or any media in the Library by clicking on the title and selecting Rename.

The text box containing the name at the bottom of the thumbnail will become accessible, and you can type in the new name. Click Enter when finished.

Alternatively, click the name portion of the thumbnail once, wait a moment, and then click this area again and the name text will become accessible for typing. Press Enter when finished.

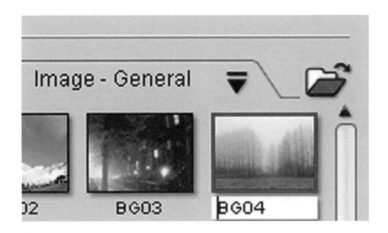

Adding Video Frames to the Library

You may add any frame of a video to the Library after capture. Sometimes it's nice to use a still capture for a menu button or background.

Use the playback controls or counter to move the slider in the Jog Bar to the frame you want to add to the Library.

From the Video Options Control Panel select the Add Current Frame to Library icon.

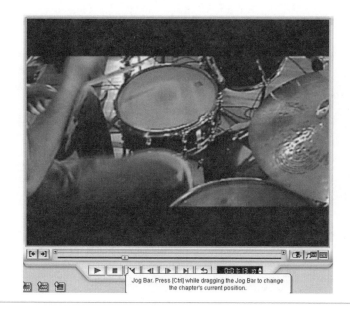

Add Current Frame to Library

Insert current frame displayed in the Preview Window to the Image Library

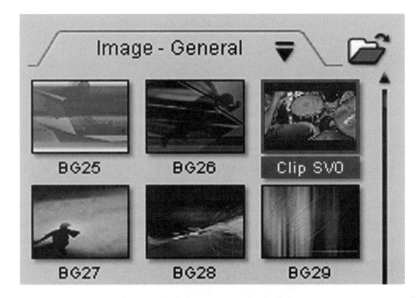

The frame is added to the Images – General Library folder.

Creating a Slideshow

From the Edit screen, you can create a slideshow, or a sequence of still images, to be played back on a DVD player. Slideshows may be mixed with video on the same DVD.

How Do I Create a Slideshow?

Add an image to be used in the slideshow from the Library to the Title List by either clicking on it and selecting Add to Title List or by dragging the image to the Title List.

Remember, you can also click the Import Image icon above the Title List to import an image directly to the Title List.

In order to invoke the slideshow function of DVD Workshop, you must place additional images *directly on top* of the first image you added to the Title List. You may add them one at a time or select multiple images by holding the Control key while selecting. Notice the icon in the lower-left portions of the thumbnail indicating a slideshow

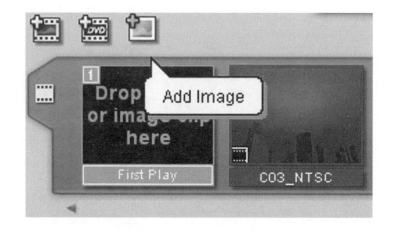

Arranging the Image Order and Adjusting Images

As images are added to the Title List you will see each one added as a thumbnail to the Chapter List. You can rearrange the order of the chapters (images) by dragging them to new positions in the Chapter List.

Double-click any image except the first one in the Chapter List to enable all options functions in the image tab of the Options panel. Another way to arrange the image order is to select the Arrange Images icon in the Image Options panel.

Select multiple images in the library by pressing Control and clicking each image, then dragging the group of images to the Title List.

Project 2.dws (3.5 MB)

Image   Audio   Subtitle

Total duration: 28   sec(s)

Add Transition

B   Random

0   sec(s)

90   90

4   sec(s)

Arrange Images

Images may be arranged from the Arrange Images dialog. Hold and click to drag images from one location to another.

From Image Options you can rotate and delete images selected in the Chapter List. You may also change the duration each image is displayed. The total length of the slideshow is displayed at the top of the Image Options area. For this slideshow, seven images multiplied by four seconds per image equals 28 seconds total.

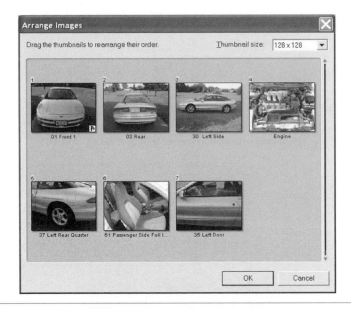

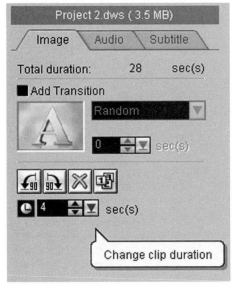

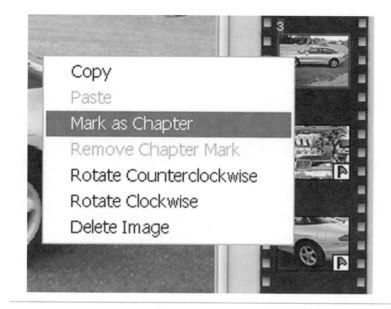

Setting Images as Chapters

Images may be set as chapters by right-clicking on them in the Chapter List or Arrange Images dialog and selecting the Mark as Chapter option. The small flag icon in the lower-left portion of the nhumbnail indicates that the image is a chapter. Chapters can be directly accessed from the DVD remote control.

Workshop allows random transitions to be inserted. This is an easy tool that will instruct Workshop 2.0 to choose what transitions occur between slides.

Adding Transitions to Slideshows

A transition is an effect used to transform one image into the next. They are best used with discretion. Click the Add Transition checkbox to add transitions to the slideshow. Then select a transition type from the drop-down menu and the duration for the transitions. Transition selections apply to all images in the slideshow.

Adding Audio to a Slideshow

Select the slideshow you want to add audio to by double-clicking on it in the Title List or selecting it in the Chapter List.

For a DVD Project:

Select the Audio tab in the Options panel and select the "Add audio track" icon.

Navigate to the audio file you wish to use, select it and press Open.

For a VCD or SVCD Project:

Click the Background Music box in the Options panel to open the Load Audio File dialog. Navigate to the desired audio file and select Open.

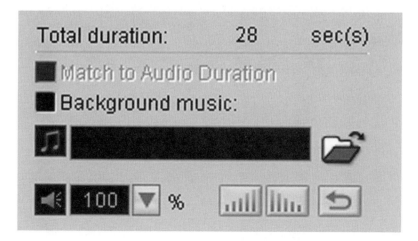

Can I Preview My Slideshow?

One of the primary upgrades in DVD Workshop 2.0 is real-time preview. This saves a lot of time. To preview the slideshow, click the Menu tab at the top of the screen. Drag the first thumbnail in the Chapter List into the Preview window. Alternately, you may drag the slideshow to the Preview window from the Title List.

Click the Finish tab at the top of the screen. Click the play button in the remote and then click the image in the Preview window. That's it! Your slideshow will begin to play.

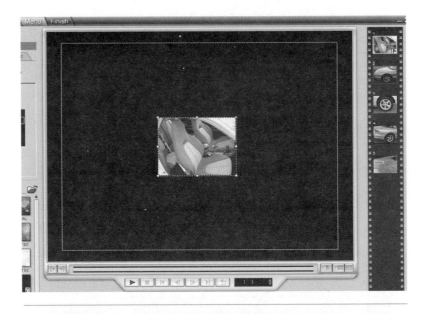

Setting a Title for First Play

A first-play video is a title that will play as soon as your DVD is inserted into a DVD player or loaded into a software media player. When the first-play video finishes, the Main Menu will be displayed.

This is a good place to have a copyright notice show on your video, or a video that displays your company logo or message.

Any title (video, slideshow, or image) may be used as a first-play video.

You can preview your first-play video by clicking the Finish tab and then clicking the Play button in the simulated remote control.

To remove the first-play video, click the first-play video thumbnail and select Remove First Play Video from the pop-up menu. Alternatively, you may select the First Play video and press the Delete key.

Select the Force First Play option in the audio control panel when the first-play video is selected if you want to remove the viewer's option to fast-forward or skip your first-play video.

Working with Audio

Inserting and Replacing Audio Tracks

In order to work with the audio of a title you must select the title for editing by double-clicking the title thumbnail or right-clicking it and selecting Edit. The Audio tab of the Options panel will become active.

If the title does not have an audio track, you can add one by clicking the "Add audio track" icon.

Browse to the audio file you want to use for the title from the Load Audio File dialog box and click "Open" after you have selected the file. You can preview the audio file by selecting the play icon at the bottom of this dialog.

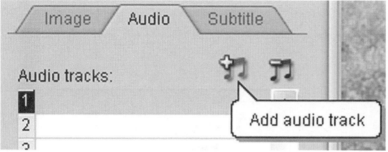

If you would like to replace the audio track associated with a title with another audio file, you must first delete the current audio track. Select the audio track in the Audio Options panel and click the "Remove audio track" icon or press the Delete key.

Monitor each video's audio in Finish mode to help determine if there are differences in level that need to be adjusted.

Adjusting Audio Track Volume

To adjust the audio track volume, click the Adjust Volume drop-down menu and drag the volume-control slider. If there is more than one audio track present be sure to select the track you want to adjust by first highlighting it, since each audio track can have a preset volume level.

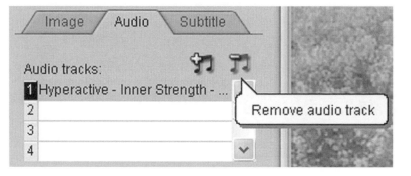

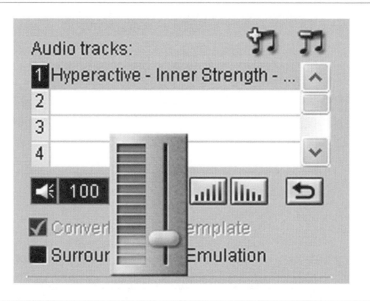

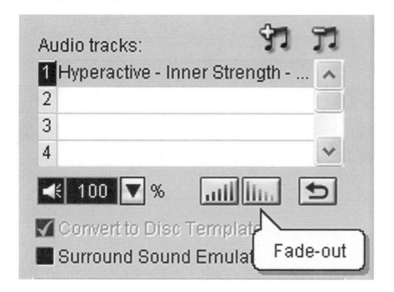

Fading In and Fading Out Audio Tracks

Audio tracks may be faded in and out so that they do not start or end abruptly. To fade in or out an audio track, select the track and select the fade-in icon or the fade-out icon.

A quick fade might be useful if there is a pop or other noise at the start or end of a video track.

When Would I Want to Fade In or Fade Out an Audio Track?

For example, if your title video is exactly two minutes long and your selected audio track for this title is three minutes long, then the audio will abruptly be cut off as the video ends at the two-minute point. Selecting Fade-out will allow the audio to slowly reduce in level at the end of the title.

Can I Change the Fade In or Fade Out Duration?

Yes, the Fade In and Fade Out duration can be adjusted from Global Settings>P references>Default Settings tab. There is also a setting here to have all of the audio in your project automatically Fade In and Fade Out, although it is probably best to make this decision for each title.

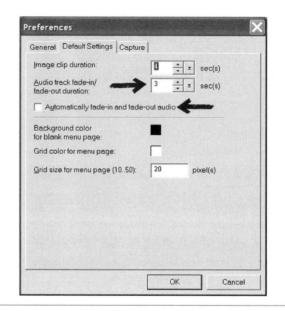

Looping Audio

If "Loop audio" is selected, then the currently selected audio track will loop until the title it is associated with stops playing. For example, if the title is five minutes long and the audio track is two minutes long, then the audio track will play two-and-a-half times (2   2.5 = 5).

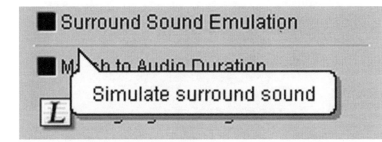

Surround Sound Emulation

The Surround Sound Emulation feature attempts to recreate the 5.1 speaker output from a two-channel (stereo) source. This effect will be heard only on multi-channel audio hardware and should be tested before committing to the final DVD. It is intended to be used with stereo sources that were down-converted from multi-channel 5.1 audio.

Adding Chapters to a Title

Adding Chapters Using I-Frames

As discussed in the beginning of this chapter it is recommended that "Locate I-frame" be selected in the Video Options panel when adding chapters to a title. Remember that you must have a video title selected to access the Video Options panel.

Using the playback controls or the counter, select a location in a video title where you would like to create a chapter point. A chapter is a point in the video title that can be directly accessed by the viewer.

Click the Add Chapter icon in the Video Options panel.

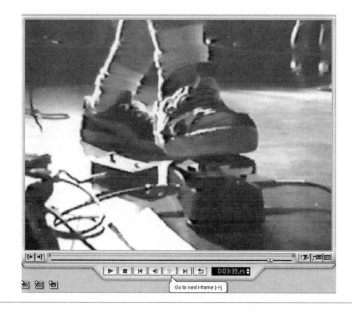

Insert current frame as chapter in the Chapter List [A]

There is also an Add Chapter icon to the right of the playback controls.

The new chapter will be added to the Chapter List. Subsequent chapters will be added to the Chapter List in chronological order. Holding the mouse over a chapter brings up an information balloon showing the chapter's location in the title.

Video chapter
Timecode: 00:03:39.25

How Do I Change a Chapter Thumbnail Image?

Use this feature to create a graphic that may be used for a video that has a black starting frame. The thumbnail may then be used to link to the video, but the button won't have a black screen at the start.

If the default thumbnail for the chapter (first frame of the chapter) does not reflect the chapter's contents, you may use any frame in the video title to which the chapter belongs. Move the slider in the Jog Bar to the video frame you want to use, click the chapter, and select Set Chapter Thumbnail.

Automatically Adding Chapters

You can automatically add all of the chapters in a video title to the Chapter List using the Scene Detection function. Select the Auto Add Chapter icon in the Video Control panel.

Click Scan. All detected scenes with selected checkboxes will be added to the Chapter List.

Working with Disc Templates for Best Results

If you select a title video you may see if it is compliant with the current disc template by looking at the status of the Convert to Disc Template dialog in the Video Options panel of the Edit screen.

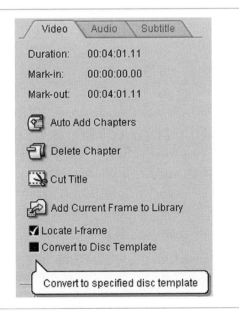

Will My Video Titles Be Re-Rendered?

There are three possible states for this dialog:

Re-rendering, or "recompressing" an already compressed file will cause significant degradation of the original file, particularly with highly compressed formats such as MPEG.

1. The dialog is available and not checked. This means that the video clip is compliant with the disc template and will not be re-rendered upon the Finish step. This option is optimal and will keep your MPEG at its original quality.

2. The dialog is available and you have checked it. This means that the video clip is compliant with the current disc template but you want to re-render it upon the Finish step. This is something that is not recommended unless absolutely necessary to fit the project on the disc.

■ Convert to Disc Template

✓ Convert to Disc Template

3. The dialog is grayed out (not available.) In this case you have no choice; the video clip is not compliant with the disc template and must be re-rendered. Remember that all non-MPEG-2 files will have to be encoded for DVD projects. If the original source file is an AVI or a digital video .mov, quality will not be tremendously affected. If the original source is WMV or other highly compressed source, expect some loss of image quality.

Will My Audio Files Be Re-Encoded?

You may also check to see if audio files are compliant by selecting them (or the video clip to which they are associated), and then checking the "Convert to specified disc template" checkbox in the Audio Options panel of the Edit screen.

Disc Template Recommendations

AC3, or Audio Compression 3, is a compression scheme that allows very high-quality audio to fit on a disc as an alternative to uncompressed audio. The lesser space used by AC3-compressed audio provides greater space for higher-quality video.

Remember that you can convert the audio stream of a clip without re-rendering the video stream or vice-versa. For example, if a DVD project includes a video clip with a compliant MPEG-2 video stream and a compliant LPCM audio stream, it would be advantageous to convert the audio stream to AC3 audio to save disc space.

If you are having trouble with DVD Workshop seeing your video title as compliant, check Table 2.1 for inconsistencies. Also remember that the video bitrate for DVD and SVCD projects must be equal to or less than the disc template's bitrate setting in order for the video title to be compliant.

Format	Frame Rate (fps)	Supported Resolutions	Video Bitrate (kbps)	Audio Properties
NTSC DVD	29.97	720x480, 704x280, 352x480, 352x240	CBR/VBR 1777-8264	LPCM Stereo, MPEG* (64-384kbps), Dolby Digital (64-448kbps) all at 48000Hz
PAL DVD	25	720x576, 704x576, 352x576, 352x288	CBR/VBR 1777-8264	LPCM Stereo, MPEG* (64-384kbps), Dolby Digital (64-448kbps) all at 48000Hz
NTSC VCD	29.97	352x240	CBR 1150	MPEG, 44100Hz, Stereo, Joint Stereo, Dual Channel, 224kbps
PAL DVD	25	352x288	CBR 1150	MPEG, 44100Hz, Stereo, Joint Stereo, Dual Channel, 224kbps
NTSC SVCD	29.97	480x480	CBR/VBR 192-2600	MPEG, 44100Hz, Stereo, Joint Stereo, Dual Channel, 64-384kbps
PAL SVCD	25	480x576	CBR/VBR 192-2600	MPEG, 44100Hz, Stereo, Joint Stereo, Dual Channel, 64-384kbps

*MPEG is not part of the NTSC DVD specification but most players decode this audio format

Deciphering Output Display Options

What Are Output Display Options?

Output Display Options are provided so that you may choose how each video title in your project is displayed on a TV that is not the same aspect ratio as the video title. This occurs when a 4:3 video title is displayed on a 16:9 TV or when a 16:9 (widescreen) video title is displayed on a 4:3 TV. The Output Display Options dialog is accessed by right-clicking a title in the Title List.

The Output Display Options dialog shows the aspect ratio of the selected title and provides output options for displaying video titles in different aspect ratios and levels of zoom.

Set the Preview Window Aspect Ratio

Before deciding on the Output Display Options for titles, set the Preview window to the aspect ratio the project is intended to be viewed in. The aspect ratio of the Preview window can be selected from the icon located at the bottom right of the Preview window in the Edit screen.

Settings for 4:3 Titles Viewed on 16:9 TVs

The As Is option will direct the DVD player to display video titles at a 4:3 aspect ratio upon playback. The entire image will be displayed on the screen with black pillars on either side of the image. Use this option if you want to see the entire 4:3 video title at the correct aspect ratio on a 16:9 screen.

The Source is Letterboxed option will direct the DVD player to display video titles with a 4:3 aspect ratio so that they are zoomed to fill the entire 16:9 TV screen upon playback with the top and bottom of the image cropped out. Use this option if your video title has black bars at the top and bottom or if you want view your 4:3 video title to fill the entire 16:9 screen at the proper aspect ratio.

The Stretch option will direct the DVD player to stretch 4:3 video title to fill a 16:9 screen upon playback. Although the entire image will be displayed, it will appear to be stretched horizontally

The Keep Aspect Ratio option will direct the DVD player to display video titles at the aspect ratio determined by the video title's resolution. 720 480 video titles will be displayed at an aspect ratio of 3:2 while 640 480 video titles will be displayed at an aspect ratio of 4:3.

The Keep Aspect Ratio (no pillarbox) option will direct the DVD player to display video titles in the same manner as the Keep Aspect Ratio option described above except that the image will be zoomed to fill the entire 16:9 screen so that the top and bottom of the image is cropped.

Settings for 16:9 Titles Viewed on 4:3 TV's

The Letterbox Only option will direct the DVD player to display 16:9 video titles at the correct aspect ratio on a 4:3 screen. The entire image will be displayed with black bars at the top and bottom of the image.

The Pan & Scan option will direct the DVD player to display 16:9 video titles at the correct aspect ratio on a 4:3 screen. The image will be zoomed so that it fill the entire 4:3 screen with a horizontal portion of both the left and right side of the image being cropped out.

Pan and Scan could potentially cause video to become pixilated depending on the quality of the image after compression. Be aware that without high-quality video going in, Pan and Scan could compromise some image quality.

The Both Letterbox and Pan & Scan option will direct the DVD player to recognize and properly display the Letterbox and Pan & Scan portions of the video title that has been so encoded.

Chapter 3

What's on the Menu?

Creating menus is one of the powers of DVD authoring. All of the previous lessons have been leading toward actually creating menus for your projects.

Menu creation is at the heart of DVD Authoring. In the menu screen you will learn how to link objects and text to titles to create buttons. In addition, playlists, one of the most powerful features of DVD Workshop 2.0, are also created and adjusted in the menu screen. You may also use hidden buttons, animated objects, highlight images, motions menus, background music, motion objects, and a variety of other decorative elements to make your menus not only extremely user friendly, but also artistic statements that complement the theme of your project.

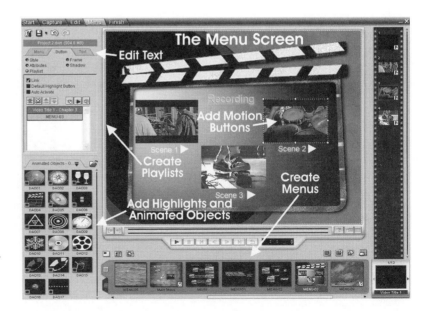

Using the Menu Wizard to Create Menus

What Is the Logic Behind the Menu Wizard?

The first step to using the Menu Wizard is to load all of your media into the Title List with chapter points set. The screenshot displays a project named Video Title 1 containing four chapters, Video Title 2 containing three chapters, and Slideshow containing six images. Let's see how the Menu Wizard handles these titles.

Select the Create Menu - Wizard icon to start the Menu Wizard. You may also press Alt+W.

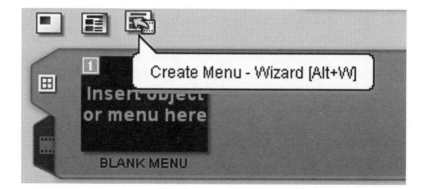

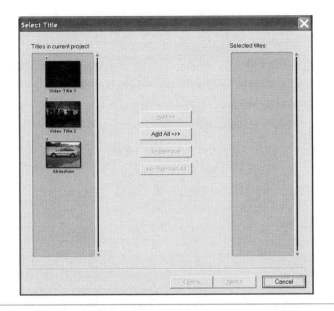

Select the titles that you would like the Menu Wizard to include in the project. In this sample project we are going to include all three titles so we can see how the Menu Wizard deals with them. Select Add All, and the titles will move to the Selected Titles pane of this dialog. Click OK.

The menu displayed in the Select Menu Template dialog is the first menu that will be displayed when this project is played back. Notice that this is called the Title Menu in the "Select title/ track" drop-down menu at the top of this screen, and thumbnails for all three video titles are included in this menu.

Open the "Select title/track" by selecting anywhere in the dialog. The menu will drop down and display a submenu for each of the video titles in the Main Menu. So we have learned that the Menu Wizard creates a Main Menu containing a thumbnail for each title, and a submenu for each title.

Select Video Title 1 from the "Select title/track" drop-down menu. The Menu Wizard has created a submenu for Video Title 1 that contains all four of the chapters contained in this title. What happens if a title contains more than four chapters?

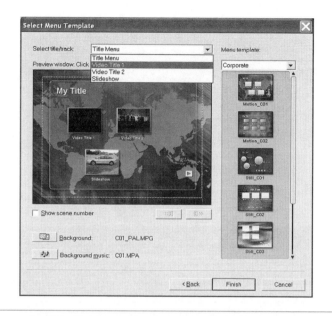

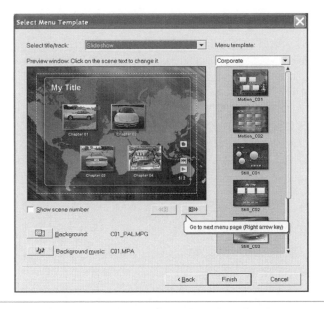

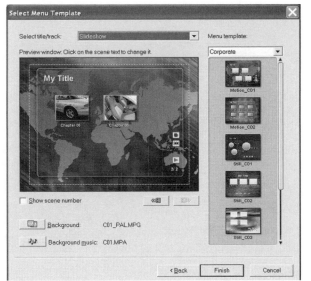

Select Slideshow from the "Select title/track" drop-down menu. The first four chapters of the Slideshow title are displayed on this submenu, but notice that the "Go to next menu page" icon is now visible.

Click the "Go to next menu page" icon at the bottom right of the menu preview window and you will see that the final two chapters of Slideshow are displayed. The Menu Wizard creates a Main Menu that includes thumbnails for all titles and a submenu for selecting scenes (chapters) for each title with enough pages to accommodate all of the scenes.

Selecting Options with the Menu Template Wizard

Menus may be named by selecting the "My Title" text and typing in a new name. If you don't change the "My Title" text then no text will appear in the final menu.

Select the "Show scene number" checkbox to number each scene (chapter) in a menu

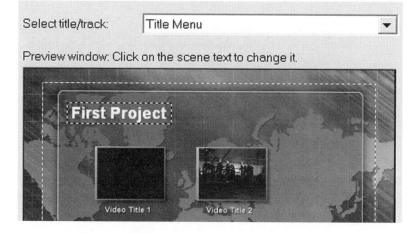

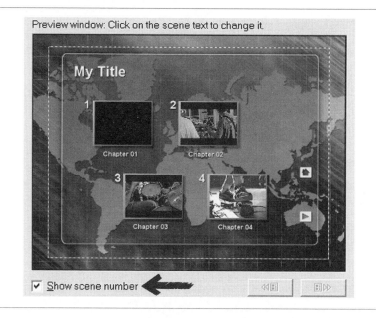

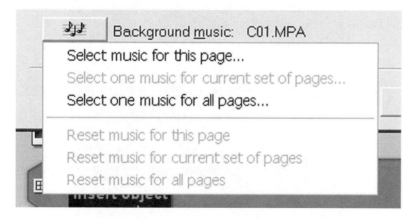

The background of a menu may be changed by clicking the Background icon. You may choose to have the background be an image or a video clip that will play when the menu is displayed (called a motion menu). These backgrounds may be selected for this menu only or for all menus currently in the Menu Wizard.

In the same manner as above, the background audio of a menu may be selected for each menu or for all of the menus in the Menu Wizard by selecting the Background Music icon and browsing to the desired audio file.

You can change the template for each menu by selecting the appropriate template from the Menu Template drop-down menu. The active menu will adopt the selected template.

Finishing the Menu Wizard

After you are satisfied with the adjustments to the Menu Wizard, click Finish. The Main Menu will be displayed in the Preview window, and all of the menus created will be displayed in the Menu List.

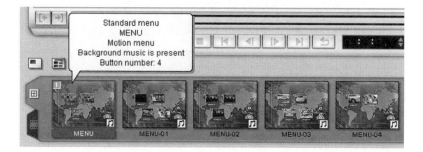

All of the menus created by the Menu Wizard can be viewed in the Menu Wizard. By holding the mouse over a menu some attributes of the menu are displayed. Each selectable link on a menu is called a button.

Using Templates to Create Menus

Selecting a Menu Template

Although creating menus using templates can be more time-consuming than using the Menu Wizard, it also provides greater creative flexibility. Click the Create Menu – Template icon or press Alt+T.

The Menu Wizard is terrific for getting a DVD built quickly and with high quality. Even professional menu authors use the Wizard when time is of the essence. Wizards are great tools for learning layout and design as well.

Choose a menu template from the Select Menu Template dialog and click Finish. Thumbnail menus use thumbnail images (also called graphic objects) as buttons while text menus use linked text as buttons.

The selected menu template will appear in both the Preview window and the Menu List.

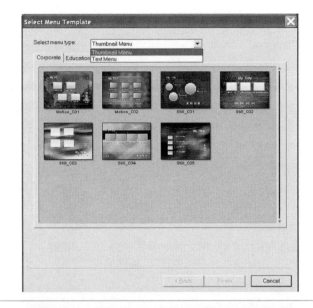

Menu templates may also be selected from the Library. Click the Down Arrow icon to open the drop-down Library menu. Choose a menu template category.

Select a menu template by right-clicking a menu and clicking Add to Menu List or drag the menu template to the Preview window.

The Menu/Title List

Navigate to the Menu Screen. You'll notice that there are two tabs on the left side of the Menu List that are not available in the Capture or Edit screens. By default the Menu List is displayed, but by selecting the lower tab you may also access the Title List while working in the Menu screen.

How Do I Link a Video Clip to a Button?

A link is an association between a button and a video clip. When a button is selected, the media associated, or linked, with the button is played. This is much like the hyperlinked text used all the time with Internet browsers. Drag Title from the Title List onto a button to create a link.

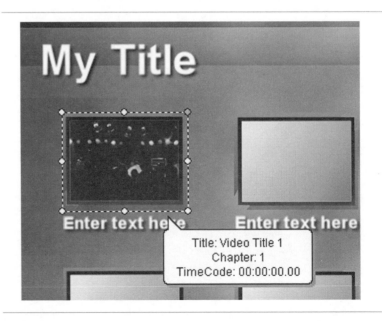

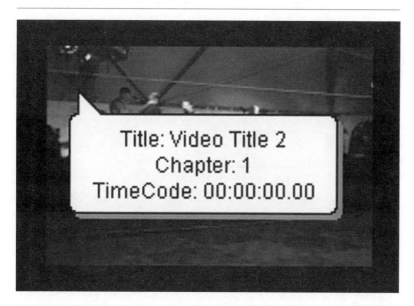

How Do I Remove a Link?

A link may be removed by navigating to Menu>Options Panel>Menu Tab>Playlist and unchecking the Link checkbox.

How Can I Determine What an Object Is Linked to?

If the cursor is over a linked object a pop-up dialog displaying information about the media the object is linked to will appear.

The button information for all linked objects in the menu can also be displayed by clicking the Show/Hide Button Information icon. This icon is located at the bottom right of the Preview window.

The name of the linked title is displayed along with the chapter number and the timecode location of the chapter for all buttons in the menu.

While it is tempting to leave this button enabled, the information balloons can quickly become overlaid, hiding the Preview window. Leaving it off until you need it is a recommended practice.

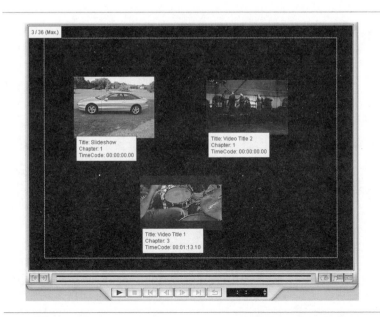

Removing Graphics Objects from a Menu

Graphic objects such as buttons and text may be removed from menus by selecting them and pressing the Delete key or by right-clicking on the object and selecting Delete from the pop-up menu.

How Do I Link an Object to Another Menu?

Let's create a scene selection menu, or a submenu for the Main Menu just as the Template Wizard did in the previous section. Create another menu using the Menu Template and name it "SubMenu." Name the first menu "Main Menu." As with naming titles, you can right-click the menu and select Rename to name the menu.

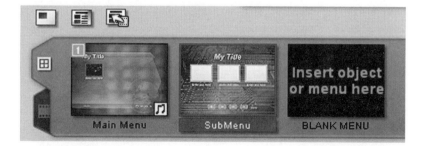

Drag a chapter into a button in Sub-Menu to create a link to the chapter. Three chapters have been linked in this example. The thumbnail images for the chapter are displayed in the button.

Select (double-click) Main Menu so that it appears in the Preview window.

With the button tab of the Options panel active, drag an image into Main Menu. This object will be our linked object. Menus can be linked to graphic objects in the same manner that titles are linked to graphic objects. Instead of media playing, a menu is displayed.

Drag SubMenu from the Menu List and drop it onto the newly created object (the image). Once linked the object is a referred to as a button, If you hover the cursor over the button, "Menu: Sub-Menu" will be displayed in pop-up text. This means that this button is linked to a menu called "SubMenu." The link is verified.

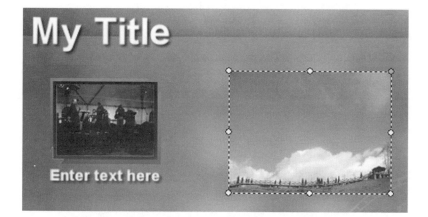

Notice that the thumbnail image in the Menu List reflects any changes made to the menu in the Preview window. Hovering the cursor over a menu in the Menu List displays a balloon with information about the menu.

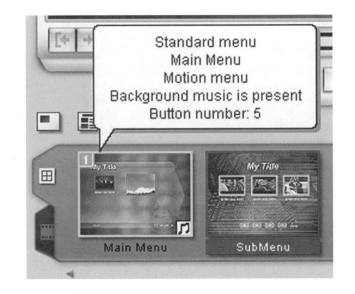

Creating and Working with Blank-Menus

Starting with a blank menu is the most flexible way to author a DVD project. It can also be the most time-consuming since you have to add any background videos or images, graphic objects, audio, or other effects to the menu. Click the Create Menu - Blank icon to create a blank menu

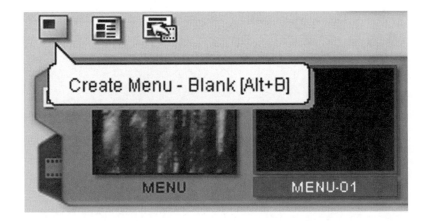

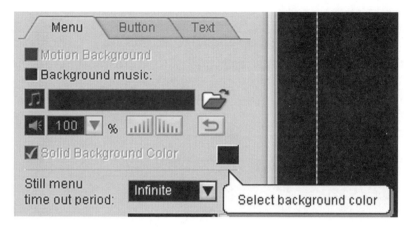

The background color of a blank menu can be changed by selecting the "Select background color" icon in the Menu tab of the Options panel.

You may pick a color from the selection of preset colors or create a custom color using either the Ulead or Windows color picker.

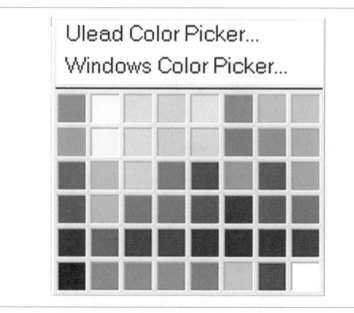

Setting the Default Blank Menu Background Color

The default color for a blank menu is black, but it can be changed in the Global Settings>Preferences>Default Settings tab.

Adding Background Images to a Menu

The same image can either be used as a background image or a graphic object in a menu depending on the state of DVD Workshop when the image or graphic is moved into the menu. Loading image BG02 into the Preview window while the Options panel Menu tab is selected will load BG02 as a background image.

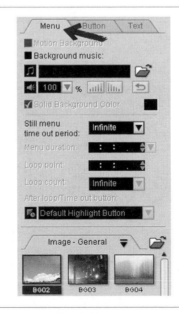

The image is now the background image for the previously blank menu.

Adding a Graphic Object (Button) to a Menu

Let's add the same image to the menu but this time first select the Button tab from the Options panel before dragging the image from the Library to the Preview window.

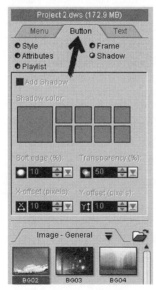

The same image is now a graphic object, or button, and can be linked to media or menus.

Alpha-channel objects can only be imported into the Objects library for their transparency to work. Ulead's UFO and Adobe's PSD files can be multi-layered, and each layer becomes a separate object in the workspace.

Restoring a Solid Background Color to a Menu

A solid background color can be restored to a menu that has a background image applied by selecting the Solid Background Color checkbox in the Options panel Menu tab.

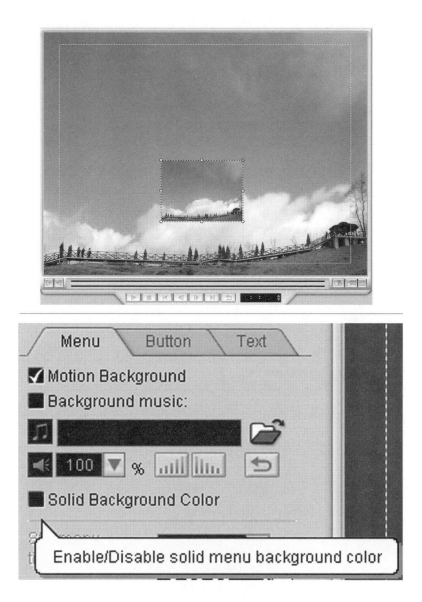

Importing Graphic Objects

Graphics objects that contain alpha-channel information can be imported into the Library if the button tab is selected in the Control Panel. Acceptable file types include Ulead File For Objects (UFO) and Photoshop (PSD) files.

Text in Menus

Text in menus is managed from the Text tab of the Options panel.

How Do I Insert and Position Text in a Menu?

Text is inserted into a menu by double-clicking on the menu where the text is to be located. The cursor will appear, and text may be entered. To close the open text dialog click anywhere outside of the dialog.

A text box may be moved broadly around the menu by dragging the text box. The arrow keys may be used for fine adjustments.

Inserting Text in a Menu is |

A text box may be positioned by dragging the text box. The keyboard up/down, left/right keys are used for fine positioning.

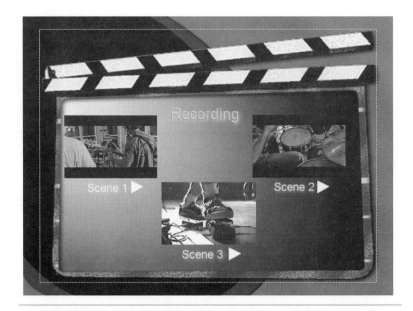

Keeping Text Within the Safe Title Area

The dotted red line around the perimeter of the Preview window is called the title-safe area. It represents the portion of the screen that will be displayed when the project is played on a TV. It's a good idea to keep important objects, such as text, well within the title-safe area.

Because the title-safe area varies from TV to TV depending on the overscan settings, and each user may wish to work with different tolerances, the title-safe area may be adjusted from the Global Settings>Preferences>General tab.

How Do I Use Text as a Link (in a Menu?

Text is linked to a title using the same methods as any button. Drag and drop the selected title directly onto the text box you want linked. The status of the link may be checked by viewing the Playlist dialog of the Text tab in the Options panel.

Formatting and Scaling Text

The text font, size, style (bold, italic, underline), justification, and text color may be adjusted from the Panel Options>Text tab. Select the text box to be formatted and make the necessary adjustments.

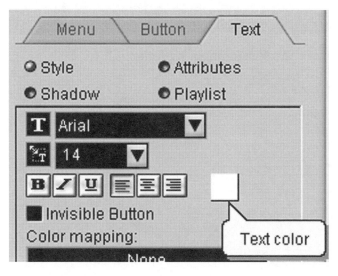

Text can be proportionally scaled by dragging any corner handle. Vertical or horizontal non-proportional scaling is accomplished by dragging the nodes in the middle of each edge of the text box.

What Is an Action State?

The color-mapping area of the Text tab determines the color of linked text when the cursor rolls over or selects the text. This is referred to as an action state. The left color of a pair of colors is the rollover color; the right color is the color the linked text turns when the text is clicked.

Stretch text or images from the middle nodes to create unusual or creative looks, fill empty spaces, or to create dramatic images. Use the transparency found in the Attributes panel to reduce opacity of text or images.

Customizing Color Mapping (DVD Projects Only)

The color-mapping attributes of linked text may be customized by clicking Customize at the bottom of the Color Mapping dialog. Keep in mind that linked text is a specific type of button, which is itself a specific type of graphic object.

The rollover and selected text colors may be changed by selecting the appropriate color to customize and either typing in RGB values or dragging the cursor around the color space. All buttons, including linked text on the screen, will turn to the selected color in the Preview window Color Mapping dialog box.

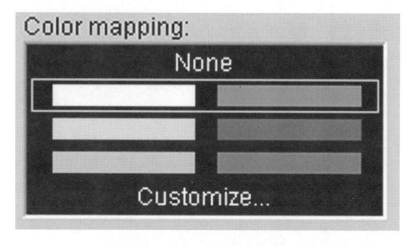

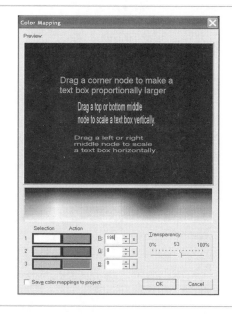

Transparency

0%   53   100%

☐ Sav̲e color mappings to project

The Transparency slider controls how transparent the color on top of the button image will be. At 100 percent transparency, no color will be evident. At 0 percent transparency, no button image will be evident, only the selected color.

As of a late beta version of DVD Workshop 2.0, this button is included but has no function. All changes to color mappings will be applied to the current project and saved with the project if the project is saved.

Adding Shadows to Text

Shadows can be added to text from the shadow options of the Text tab in the Options panel.

After selecting the text that you would like to apply a shadow, click the Add Shadow checkbox.

The "Soft edge" setting controls the amount of focus of the shadow.

X-offset and Y-offset specify the location of the shadow. A X-offset of 0 and a Y-offset of 0 would place the shadow directly behind the text. The shadow offset may also be adjusted in real time in the Preview window by selecting the text, clicking the Add Shadow checkbox and dragging the shadow bounding box node. This node is green.

Soft Edge at 1%, Transparency at 50%

Soft Edge at 5%, Transparency at 50%

Soft Edge at 10%, Transparency at 50%

Adjusting X and Y Shadow Offset in the Preview Window

Drag this node to adjust X and Y Offset

A shadow may be removed by either right-clicking the graphic object with the shadow and selecting Remove Shadow or by unchecking the Remove Shadow checkbox in the Text tab>Shadow Options panel.

Adjusting Text Brightness, Contrast, and Transparency

Brightness, contrast, and transparency of text can be adjusted from the Attributes options of the Text tab in the Options panel. Remember that a text box must be selected for these options to be available.

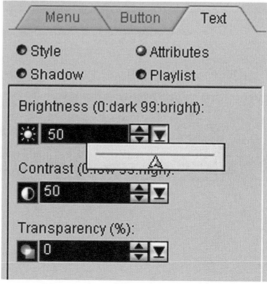

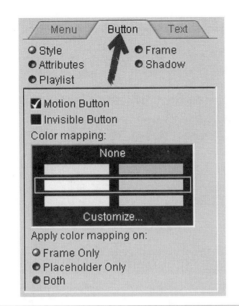

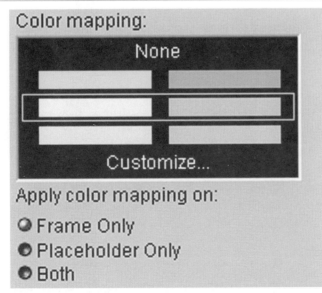

Working with Graphic Objects

Graphic objects can be customized from the button tab of the Menu Options panel. Also keep in mind that text boxes are graphic objects and that many of the features in this section can be used with text.

Adjusting the Color Mapping of Buttons (DVD Projects Only)

The colors of the mouse rollover and mouse select action states for objects are adjusted from the Color Mapping dialog in the same manner as with text buttons. If the button has a frame, then the color mapping of the frame and placeholder (thumbnail area) may be individually set.

Adjusting Brightness, Contrast, and Transparency

Brightness, contrast, and transparency of graphic objects can be adjusted from the Attributes options of the Button tab in the Options panel. Remember that a graphic object must be selected for these options to be available.

How Do I Rotate a Graphic Object?

A graphic object may be rotated by selecting the object and typing in the degree of rotation into the Rotation field located at Options Panel>Button tab>Attributes. The rotation slider may also be used to set a value.

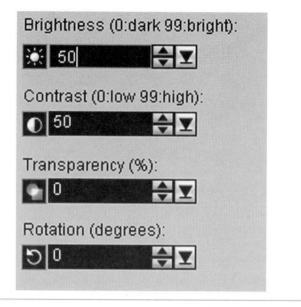

You may also rotate a graphic object by dragging the top-right node (the one that is not yellow) of a selected graphic object clockwise or counter-clockwise.

How Do I Scale a Graphic Object?

A graphic object can be proportionally scaled by dragging any corner node except the top-right corner node. Non-proportional horizontal and vertical scaling is accomplished by dragging middle the nodes in the middle of the each side of the box.

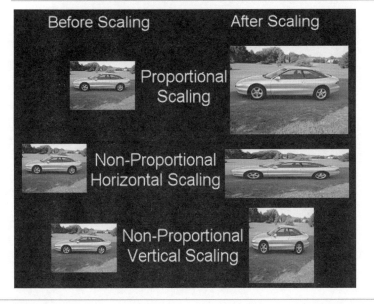

Adding a Frame to a Graphic Object

To add a frame to a graphic object first select the object to which you would like to add the frame. From the frame list at Menu Options>Button>Frame Options, either double-click the desired frame or drag it onto the graphic object.

A frame may be removed by either right-clicking the graphic object with the frame and selecting Remove Frame or selecting Remove Frame from Button>Frame Options.

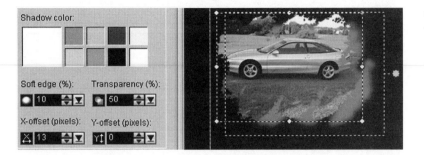

Adding a Shadow to a Graphic Object

A shadow may be added or removed to a graphic object in the exact manner as was demonstrated with text.

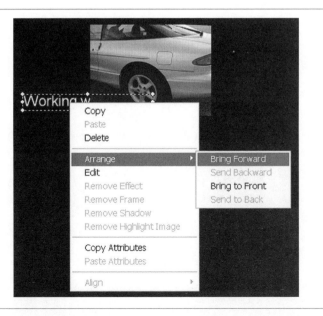

How Do I Move an Object So That It is In Front Of Another Object? (Layers)

Each graphic object occupies a different layer. To shift an object one layer forward, right-click the object and select Arrange>Bring Forward. You can also move an object to the front layer by selecting Bring to Front.

In a similar manner all objects (and text) may be moved forward or backward to different layers so that the desired objects are visible.

Copying and Pasting Objects

An object may be copied by right-clicking on the object and selecting Copy from the pop-up menu.

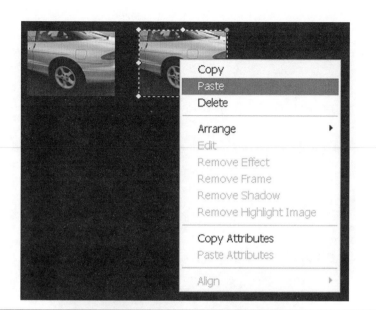

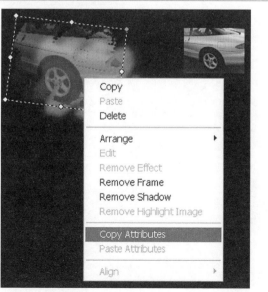

An object may be pasted by right-clicking on the object and selecting Paste from the pop-up menu. The object will be pasted at the location of the mouse cursor.

Copying and Pasting Object Attributes

Copying an object's attributes copies the object's size, color mapping, brightness, contrast, transparency, rotation (not for text), frame and shadow settings. In addition, for text objects, all text formatting will also be copied. Select the object to copy the attributes from by right-clicking on it and selecting Copy Attributes.

Right-click on the object you would
like to paste attributes to and select
Paste Attributes.

Selecting Multiple Objects

Multiple objects to be cpied or repo-
sitioned may be selected by holding
the Contral key while left-clicking each
object.

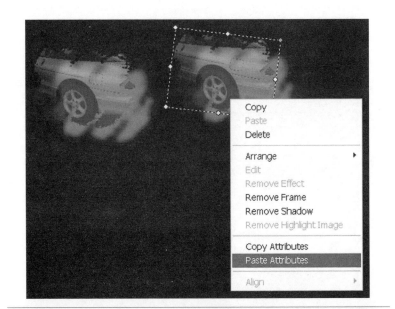

Aligning Objects

DVD Workshop provides a variety of alignment tools. Select at least two objects to be aligned using Ctrl-click and then right-click on one of the selected objects to activate the alignment options. Remember that text boxes can also be aligned!

Align Left lines up all objects so that their leftmost borders are lined up to the left side of the Preview window.

Align Top lines up all objects so that their top borders are lined up to the top of the Preview window.

Center Vertically aligns the objects so that the center of each image is positioned along an imaginary horizontal line running through all of the selected objects.

Center Both centers all of the objects so that the center point (middle) of each object is positioned at the same point. In the screenshot the layers of the objects have been adjusted so that all objects are visible. Note that this option does not center the objects to the center of the screen.

Space Evenly Horizontally/Vertically spaces all selected objects so that empty space between each object is the same.

Equal Width/Height stretches each graphic object so that they are the same width as the widest object. Selecting Equal Width and Equal Height will make all of the graphics objects the size of the largest selected object.

Using Gridlines for Menu Layout

Gridlines can be turned on by clicking the Show/Hide Gridlines icon located below and to the right of the Preview window or by pressing Alt+G.

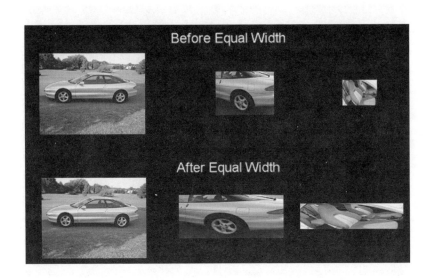

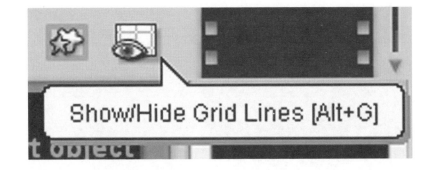

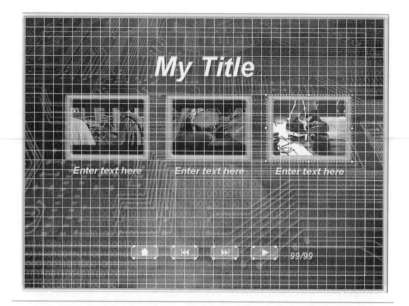

Gridlines in the Menu Preview window.

The spacing and color of the gridlines can be adjusted in Global Settings>Preferences>Default Settings.

Preferences

| General | Default Settings | Capture |

Image clip duration: `4` ⫫ sec(s)

Audio track fade-in/ fade-out duration: `3` ⫫ sec(s)

☐ Automatically fade-in and fade-out audio

Background color for blank menu page: ■

Grid color for menu page: ☐

Grid size for menu page (10..50): `20` pixel(s)

Checking Object Boundaries for Overlap

if you have overlapped buttons, DVD Workshop will display a message in the final burning preparation stages, but it's best to identify and adjust buttons before getting to that point.

It's important that object boundaries don't overlap so that there is no confusion for the DVD player when moving from button to button or selecting a button. If buttons overlap, how would the DVD player know which button to highlight when moving to the overlapped buttons?

Some objects such as those with frames have especially large boundaries. Notice that the second and third buttons do not overlap, but the first button has a shadow applied which considerably extends the object boundaries and conflicts with the second button.

Working with Playlists

Playlists—A New DVD Workshop 2.0 Feature

A playlist is a group of actions that will be carried out in sequence from the top of the list to the bottom when a Menu button is selected. Each Menu button has its own unique playlist. When the Menu button associated with the playlist shown is selected, Chapter 4 of Video Title 1 will play, and then Menu 03 will play. Graphics-button playlists are located in the Button tab, while text-button playlists are located in the Text tab.

Setting the Default Highlight Button

The Default Highlight Button checkbox allows you to select which menu button in a menu will be activated when the menu times out or or the after loop function occurs. Select the button you wish to use for this action and click the checkbox to set the default highlight button. Remember that only one button on each menu may have this option selected.

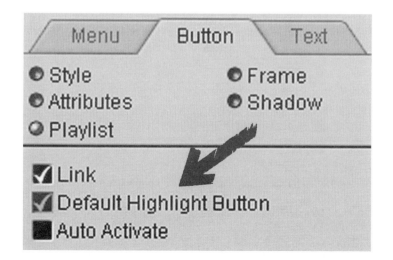

What Does Auto Activate Do?

When Auto Activate is selected for a menu button, that button will be activated when the cursor rolls over the button. This feature is most commonly used for next and previous menu page buttons.

Removing Actions from the Playlist

To remove an action from the playlist, first select the action to be removed by clicking on it. Selecting the small X icon near the left of the Playlist Options panel will remove the action. Select the large X icon to remove all actions from the playlist.

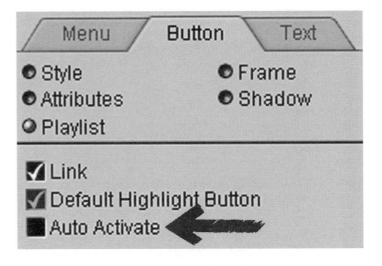

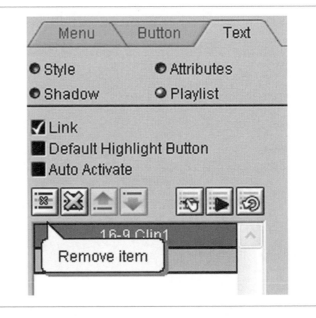

Adding a Title or Chapter to the Playlist

To add a title or chapter to the playlist, drag the thumbnail to the playlist and drop it on top of the playlist action you would like the new action be ahead of in the Playlist. In this example Slideshow has been dropped onto Main Menu.

Replacing a Menu in the Playlist

Unless a loop is set in the playlist, there must always be one menu in the playlist. To replace the current menu selection first drag and drop a menu to the playlist. Next, select Add Menu from the options that appear to replace the old menu with the new selection.

Adding a Button from a Menu to the Playlist

Drag and drop a menu into the playlist. Select Add Button from Menu from the pop-up dialog that appears. From the Custom Button dialog select the button you want to add to the playlist. The new action will take the place of the menu in the playlist since the button's playlist will contain a menu as the last action.

Arranging the Order of Actions

Select an action in the playlist and then click either the Move Up or Move Down icons to move the action up or down in the playlist sequence.

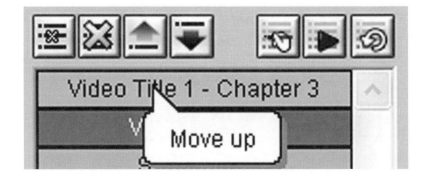

Assigning Audio and Subtitle Tracks to Titles (DVD Projects Only)

Since DVD Workshop can accommodate multiple audio and subtitle tracks for titles, you can use this dialog to assign which audio and subtitle track should be played or displayed for each title in the playlist.

Be aware that the sequence of titles in the Title List will determine the sequence of play!

Add Play All Titles (DVD Projects Only)

When "Add Play all titles" is selected, all titles in the title list will play at this point in the playlist.

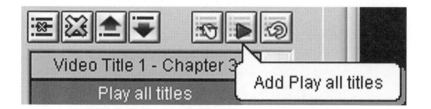

Add Start and End Loop Points (DVD Projects Only)

Clicking the "Add start and end loop points" icon adds "Loop start point" and "Loop end point" actions to the playlist. The "Loop end point" action replaces the menu normally at the end of the playlist since the looping of the playlist is infinite and returning to a menu can only occur by user command from the remote control. The "Loop start point" may be moved up and down in the playlist.

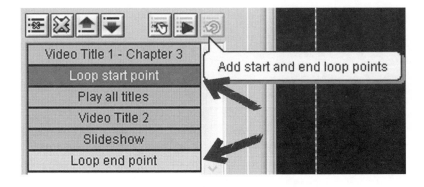

Enhancing Menus

Adding Graphics from the Ulead Library

DVD Workshop is loaded with a huge library of stock graphics and video that may be used to enhance your menus. Remember, to access these assets you must have the Menu Options panel>Button tab selected.

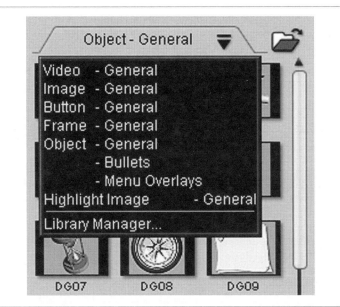

The Button Library

Here you will find a variety of buttons that can be used in your menus. You can quickly drag a button onto a menu to use it. After getting the button on the menu, it's an easy task to link a video or slideshow to the button.

In this example, triangle-shaped play buttons have been added to each scene in the menu.

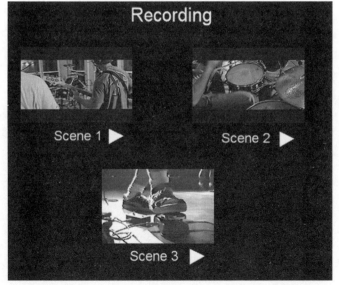

Using Frames as Menu Backgrounds

Frames can not only be used for buttons, but they can also be scaled to the size of the Preview window and used to create custom menus.

In this example a frame FR35 has been added to the menu and moved to the back layer so that the other graphic objects remain visible. The Recording style frame was selected to keep in theme with the recording motif of the clips. A text effect was also applied to the Recording text.

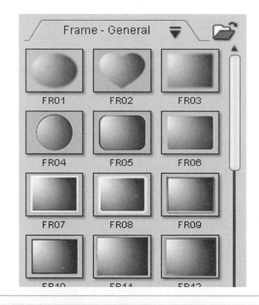

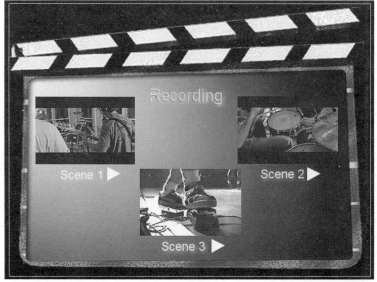

The Object Menu—General Objects

If you can't find an object in this area of the Library that fits your project remember that you can import graphics objects that have been created in other applications such as Photo Impact or Photoshop. Try as I might, I couldn't find anything here that even remotely fit this sample menu! So, I imported my own.

The Object Menu—Bullets

Ulead has included quite a variety of bullets for you to experiment with in your menu. Remember that any of the graphic objects can be used as buttons simply by adding a link.

Since a frame has been added to this menu, when bullets are added, they are scaled to the size of the frame and "framed." To avoid this, remove the frame, apply the bullets and then reapply the frame. The addition of these bullets (musical notes) has crossed the line of good taste as they are definitely drawing too much attention from the content of the menu, which are the video scenes. When in doubt, less is more.

The Objects Menu—Overlays

Parts of menu overlays are semi-transparent when on a layer on top of a graphic object and opaque (0 percent transparent) when used behind other graphic objects.

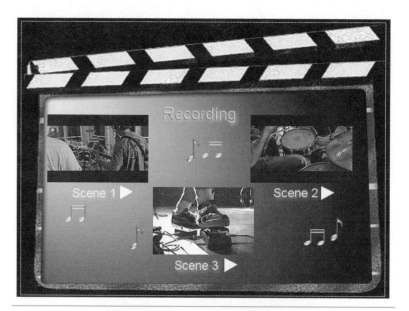

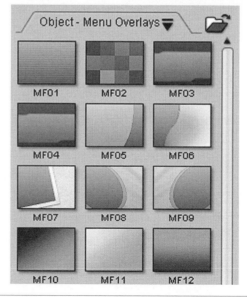

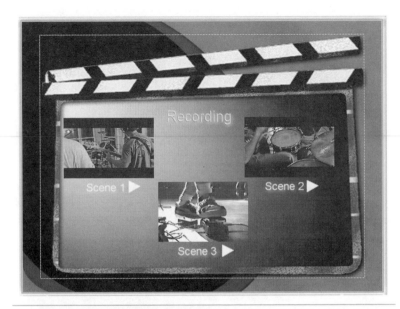

In this example the menu overlay is behind all graphic objects. Notice that it kind of fills in the empty spaces in the menu.

When the menu overlay is moved to the front layer, parts of the overlay are transparent.

What are Highlight Images? (DVD Projects Only)

When chapter points are used as buttons, the entire button thumbnail (picon, or picture icon) is highlighted when the button is in the mouse rollover state. If a highlight image is applied to the button then only the highlight image is highlighted when in the rollover state.

Using Highlight Images (DVD Projects Only)

In order to see highlight images while working with them in the Preview window click the Show/Hide Highlight Images" icon located below and to the right of the Preview window or press Alt+H.

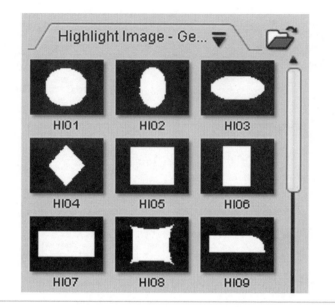

Drag and drop a highlight image onto a button. The highlight image will automatically link with the button so that even if you move the highlight image off of the button it will still become highlighted when the button associated with it is in a rollover state. The highlight image or button will activate the button if selected when it is not on the button.

Both of the buttons have highlight images applied. Notice that the left button is in a rollover state and the thumbnail is not highlighted, but the highlight image is visible. The highlight image is not visible on the other button because that button is not in the rollover state

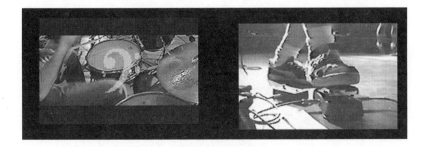

Highlight images may be scaled and rotated just like any other graphic object. Highlight images may be deleted by right-clicking on the button (but not on the highlight image) and selecting Delete Highlight Image. The highlight image may also be deleted by selecting it and pressing the Delete key.

Highlight images may also be removed by clicking the Remove Highlight Image icon located at Options panel>Button Options tab>Styles. Remember to have the button containing the highlight image selected or this option will not be visible (you may have to click the highlight image object to make this icon appear).

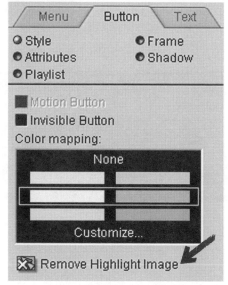

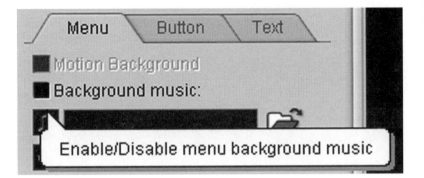

Adding Background Audio to a Menu

Background audio may be added to a menu by selecting the Background Music icon located in the Menu tab of the Options panel.

Browse to the desired audio file and select Open.

Changing the level of audio, fading in, fading out, and looping of audio is implemented in the same manner as described in Chapter 2 in the section Adding Audio to a Slideshow. A new audio file can be used by selecting the folder dialog to the right of the audio file name dialog.

Using Motion Buttons and Motion Objects (DVD Projects Only)

Motion buttons are buttons that were created from chapter or title thumbnails that will play the video associated with them when the menu is playing. Motion buttons are turned on by default and may be disabled by unchecking the Motion Button checkbox in the Options panel>Button tab>Style dialog.

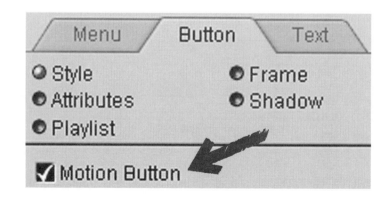

It is also possible to use a motion object or a motion button without a link. With the Button tab selected in the Options panel, add a video to the Preview window. The video will play when the menu is previewed but no link will be associated with it. The Link icon in the Playlist dialog will be grayed out for motion objects.

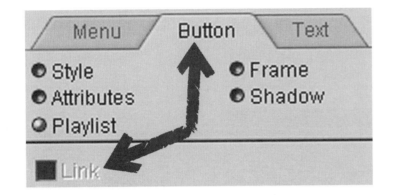

Creating a Motion Menu and Menu Time Out Actions (DVD Projects Only)

A motion menu is a background video that plays in a menu. A motion menu is applied to a menu by dragging a video from the Library onto the Preview window while the Options panel is in the Menu tab. Unchecking the Motion Background icon will disable the motion menu.

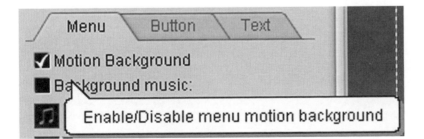

Customizing Motion Menu Playback

The Motion Menu Duration dialog sets how long the motion menu will play back before beginning to loop. If Audio Duration is selected and the audio is longer than the motion video then the motion video will loop until the audio ends.

The loop point is the time that the motion video plays from when looping. For example, if the loop point is set to 5 seconds for a 20-second motion video, then after playing once all the way through the video will begin looping the motion video from 5 seconds to 20 seconds. Click in the digits you want to enter to set a time.

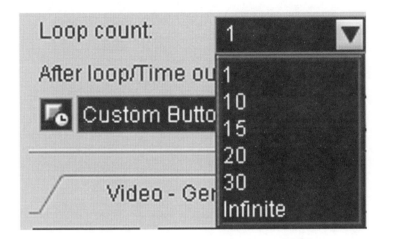

This dialog sets the number of times the motion video will loop before carrying out the After Loop/Time Out action described below. You may enter a number of loops by clicking in the Loop count dialog, entering a number, and clicking outside the field.

This dialog sets the action that occurs after the motion video has finished looping. There are two options, Default Highlight Button, which plays the button set in the Options Panel>Button tab>Playback panel, or the Custom Button option described below.

If the Custom Button option is selected the Custom Button dialog appears. Choose the video you would like to play after the looping is finished by clicking on it. Click OK when finished.

Setting the Still Menu Behavior

If a still image is used as the background for a menu and there are no motion buttons or background audio in the menu then the "Still menu time out period" dialog will be available for a time selection to be input. Set the number of seconds you would like the menu to be displayed before the After Loop/Time Out action is initiated.

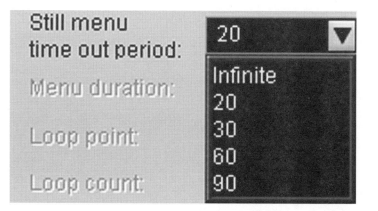

Real Time Previews from the Menu Preview Window

If your menu includes a motion menu or motion buttons you can preview the menu from the menu screen Preview window by clicking the Play icon, or pressing Enter.

The smoothness (frame rate) of Real Time Motion Menu and Motion Button previews will depend on your computer's performance and how many motion buttons are in the menu. Real-time previews are highly optimized for multithreaded systems as can be seen by the 100 percent CPU load with hyperthreading turned on.

Some motherboards and BIOS tools have difficulty with multimedia applications and hyperthreading. If you experience difficulties playing back video or with stability of multi-media applications, disable hyper-threading in your system BIOS. See the owner's manual for information on how to do this.

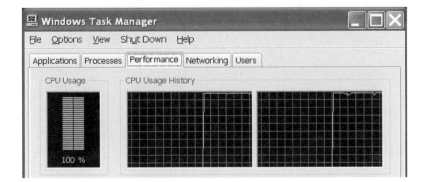

Chapter 4

Advanced Authoring Tools (DVD Projects Only)

Subtitles and multiple audio tracks are two of the new, advanced features of DVD Workshop 2.0. Both of these features are accessed from the Edit screen. Subtitles allow for text translations or assistance for hearing-impaired persons to be seen and for audio features such as foreign languages or directors' commentaries to be heard along with the original video.

Creating and Managing Multiple Audio Tracks

Every title in the title list may have as many as eight audio tracks associated with it. In order to make your production as user-friendly as possible, place the most-important audio file in Track 1 and the less-important ones on the higher numbered tracks.

What Audio Formats Will DVD Workshop Accept?

Although DVD Workshop will accept a wide variety of audio formats, remember to try and match your audio file format with the disc template so that your audio files do not need to be re-encoded. Using AC-3 formats for output of non-compliant files will greatly reduce disk space usage.

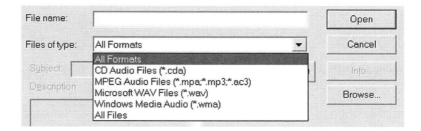

The audio properties of a video clip may be viewed by right-clicking the clip's thumbnail and selecting "Properties." If possible, try to use WAV files since they are uncompressed. Also remember to use 48kHz sampled audio files so that a sampling rate conversion isn't necessary.

Adding Audio Tracks

Select the location where you would like to add a new track by clicking the appropriate track number in the track list. If the track already contains an audio file, the new audio file will be added in its place and all files below this track will be shifted down the track list.

```
Audio
  Compression:   PCM
    Attributes:   48.000 kHz, 16 Bit, Stereo
  Total samples:  1,665,664 Samples
```

```
Video   Audio   Subtitle

Audio tracks:
1 DV Video.AVI
2
3
4
```

Select the "Add Audio Track" icon, browse to the desired track in the "Load Audio File" dialog, select the appropriate audio file, and click "OK." You may also drag an audio file to a specific audio track from the "Audio - General" folder of the Library.

Arranging and Deleting Audio Tracks

Audio tracks in the track list cannot be moved by dragging and dropping. Sometimes tracks must be deleted and readded to the track list to rearrange the order of tracks. For example, let's swap the positions of Tracks 2 and 3.

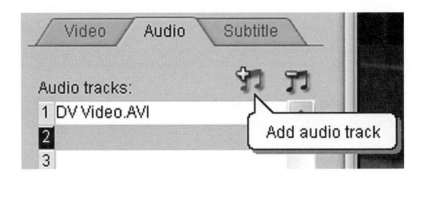

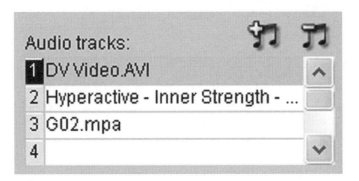

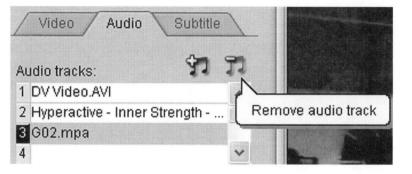

Select Track 3 by clicking on it. Delete the audio track G02.mpa by either clicking the Remove Audio Track icon or pressing the Delete key.

Drag and drop audio file G02.mpa directly onto audio Track 2. The contents of Track 2 will drop down to Track 3, and G02.mpa will be added to Track 2. The audio files in audio Tracks 2 and 3 have been switched.

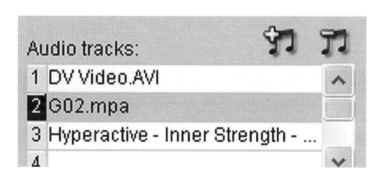

Volume, Fade, and Loop Behavior of Audio Tracks

The Volume, Fade, or Loop settings described in Chapter 2 that are selected for any highlighted track will be preserved for that track. That is, you can adjust these setting individually for each audio track in a title.

Previewing Audio Tracks with Titles Playing

You can preview any audio track in the track list while watching the corresponding video by selecting the audio track by clicking on it and playing the video. This is often useful for seeing if a particular audio tracking is enhancing or detracting from the video.

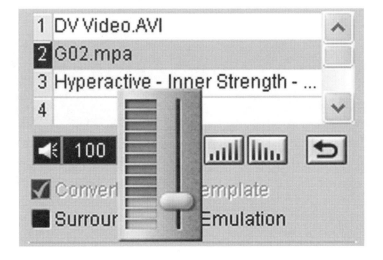

What Are Language Audio Settings?

Click the Language Settings icon in the Audio tab of the Edit screen>Control Panel.

Select an audio track by clicking on it, and select settings in the Language and Characteristics drop-down menus. These settings will be displayed by the DVD player when viewing audio options. Clicking "Apply to all titles" will apply these selections to all audio tracks associated with this title.

Creating and Managing Subtitle Tracks

Subtitles are text that appears in a video. Subtitles are edited from the Add/Edit Subtitles dialog which is accessed from the Add/Edit Subtitles icon in the Subtitles tab of the Control Panel in the Edit screen.

Subtitles are managed from the Add/Edit Subtitles dialog. Before selecting this dialog make sure you load the title you want to add subtitles to into the Edit mode by double-clicking the title.

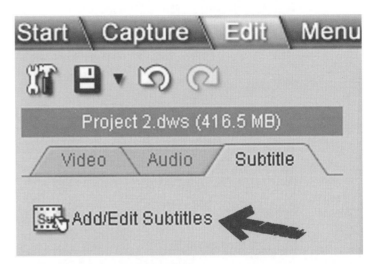

Previewing Using the Subtitle Preview Window

The Subtitle Preview window operates much the same way as the Edit Preview window except that the current subtitle track is always active; it does not have to be turned on. You may also preview any audio track associated with the title by clicking the "Switch to another audio track" icon in the bottom right of the Subtitle Preview window.

Subtitles are required if the project is federally funded, or if the project is being used for educational purposes, by the Americans with Disabilities Act.

Adding Subtitles

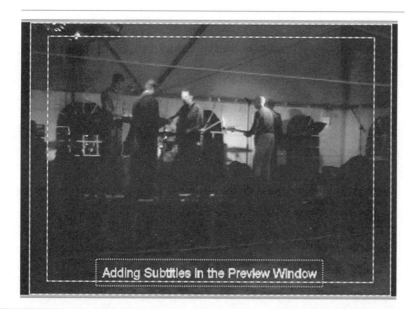

Adding Subtitles from the Preview Window

A subtitle segment may be added by clicking in the Preview window and typing text. Close the text box by clicking once outside of the text box when you are finished typing.

Adding Subtitles from the Subtitle Segment List

A subtitle segment is text that is displayed on the screen during a certain time period in the video. The Subtitle Segment List contains the start and end times that each subtitle segment will be displayed.

You may also add a subtitle segment by double-clicking the first segment in the Subtitle Segment List.

	Start	End	Subtitle
1	00:00:00.00	00:00:01.00	Adding subtitles from the Subtitle Segment List
*			

Current track: 1

	Start	End	
1	00:00:00.00	00:00:01.00	Adding Subtitles from the Subtitle Segment List
*			

Adding Subtitles from a Text File

All subtitle segments for a subtitle track are contained in a subtitle text file. Unless you learn the proper commands to manipulate subtitles in text documents, this feature is best used to reload or edit previously saved subtitle text files.

Browse to the subtitle text file, select it, and click Open. All subtitle segments will be reloaded into the Subtitle Segment List.

Specifying Start/Stop Times for Displaying Subtitle Segments

The start and stop times for displaying subtitle segments may be directly input from the Subtitle Segment List. Double-click the appropriate digit and type in the timecode. Press Enter when finished.

The mark-in and mark-out points displayed in the Preview window reflect the duration of the subtitle segment presently selected in the Subtitle Segment List. Subtitle segment durations and positions may be adjusted using mark-in and mark-out points in the same manner as trimming clips. In this example the mark-in and mark-out points reflect a subtitle segment time of 0–3 seconds on-screen time.

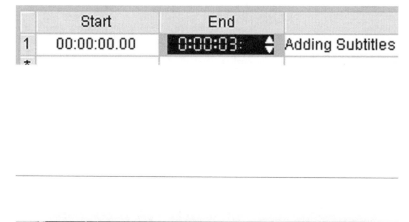

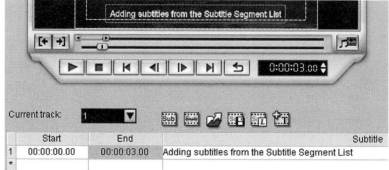

	Start	End	Subtitle
1	00:00:02.07	00:00:03.00	Adding Subtitles to Titles
2	00:00:00.00	00:00:01.15	Managing Subtitles
3	00:00:03.09	00:00:04.00	Don't overlap Subtitles Segments

Identifying Overlapping Subtitle Segments

Overlapped subtitle segments will be displayed in green in the Subtitle Segment List. The second of the two overlapping segments will be indicated by the green background. In this example Segment 2 is overlapping Segment 1.

Deleting and Inserting Subtitle Segments

You may delete a subtitle segment, delete only the text in a subtitle segment, or insert a blank subtitle segment by right-clicking on a subtitle segment and selecting the appropriate action from the pop-up menu.

	Start	End	
1	00:00:00.00	00:00:01.08	Adding Subtitles to Titles
2	00:00:01.21	00:00:02.07	Managing S Delete Segment
3	00:00:02.29	00:00:04.00	Don't overla Delete Text
*			Insert Blank Segment

Managing Subtitle Tracks

You may create up to 32 different subtitle tracks for a title. Remember that each subtitle track consists of a collection of subtitle segments. These different subtitle tracks could correspond to different audio tracks for be for different languages.

Adding and Deleting Subtitle Tracks

Subtitle tracks may be added or deleted by clicking the "Add new track" or "Delete current track" icons above the Subtitle Segment List. Because only one subtitle track can be displayed at a time, the currently active subtitle track will be deleted.

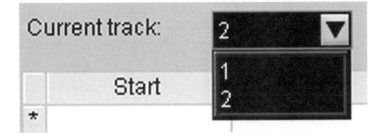

Switching Subtitle Tracks

Click the drop-down menu to select another subtitle track.

Saving Subtitle Track Information to a Text File

All of the subtitle segments that have been entered in the Subtitle Segment List, including start and stop information, text formatting, and screen positioning, will be saved in the text file. You may also edit subtitle information directly in the text file.

Current track:	1 ▼		
	Start	End	
1	00:00:00.00	00:00:02.00	Thursday, January

Save to a text file

Here are the contents of a subtitle text file that contains data for three subtitle segments.

Specifying Subtitle Language Settings

Click the "Specifying language settings" icon to open the Language Settings – Subtitle dialog box.

```
#Ulead subtitle format

#Subtitle stream attribute begin
#FR:29.97
#Subtitle stream attribute end

#Subtitle text begin
#0 00;00;00;00 00;00;01;08 X:225 Y:428
Adding Subtitles to Titles
#1 00;00;01;21 00;00;02;07 X:256 Y:428
Managing Subtitles
#2 00;00;02;29 00;00;04;00 X:180 Y:428
Don't overlap Subtitles Segments
#Subtitle text end

#Subtitle text attribute begin
#/R:1,3 /FN:Arial /CS:178 /FS:24 /AL:l /FP:8 /FC:1,1 /OC:3,1 /BC:2,16
#Subtitle text attribute end
```

Current track: 1

	Start	End	
1	00:00:00.00	00:00:02.00	Thursday, January 22,

Specify language settings

Language Settings - Subtitle ☒

Subtitle tracks list:

1	English - Caption - Normal size characters
2	English - Director's comments - Normal size characters
3	
4	
5	
6	
7	
8	

Language: English (en) ▼

Characteristics: Director's comments - Normal size characters ▼

☐ Apply to all titles

OK   Cancel

Select a subtitle track by clicking on it, and select settings in the Language and Characteristics drop-down menus. These settings will be displayed by the DVD player when viewing subtitle options. Clicking "Apply to all titles" will apply these selections to all subtitles associated with this title.

What Is Metadata?

Metadata is information embedded in digital video and digital images. This metadata can be added to a title in the form of a subtitle by clicking the "Add subtitle from metadata" icon.

Metadata is becoming common in many file types. Metadata is information about a file that is contained in that file. Metadata may consist of dates, times, tempo, musical key, copyright information, length of file, sampling rate, codec information, or descriptive information.

End	
00:00:02.00	Thursday, January 22, 2004

Add subtitle from metadata

Select the metadata you wish to include in the subtitle and the duration of the subtitle and then click OK.

A subtitle containing the metadata DV subtitle information will be created for each detected scene in the digital video title. This feature is useful for quickly time-stamping each scene of video in a title.

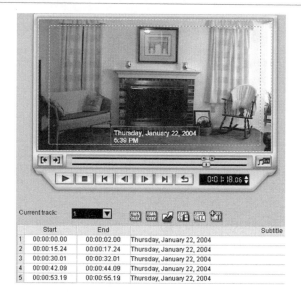

Select the EXIF information you wish to include in the subtitle and the duration of the subtitle and click OK.

A subtitle containing the EXIF information will be created for each image included in a slideshow title in the same manner that metadata information was included in each scene for DV.

Formatting Subtitle Text

The text formatting tools operate exactly the same as the text tools in the Menu screen. Select a text option, and it will automatically be displayed in the Subtitle Preview window. Here the Border effect is illustrated.

The Border effect is available only in the subtitle text formatting options. You won't find this feature in the text options panel of the Edit screen. If a background is not used for the subtitles, a darker border color around a lighter text color can help the subtitles to pop off of the image.

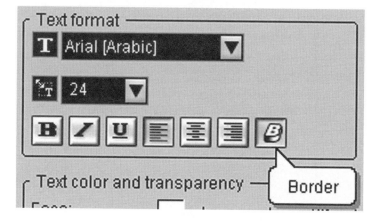

White text with a black border

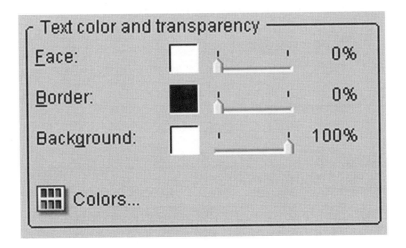

Working with Subtitle Colors

Face refers to the color of the text, Border refers to the outline color of the text when the Border effect is applied, and Background refers to the color of the rectangular background placed under the text. The transparency of these colors may also be adjusted so that the subtitles are easy to read but not distracting.

Colors for the Face, Border, and Background may be selected from the color palette by clicking the color box next to the transparency slider. Select a color from the palette.

Avoid using extreme contrasts between two colors such as placing pure white subtitles over black bars. This avoids blooming and smearing of colors. Choose light grey, off-white, or less-contrasted colors over light or dark backgrounds. This will also aid in the encoding process and render times.

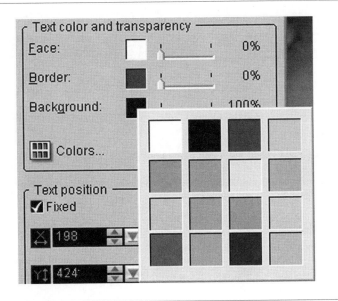

The colors in the color palette may be edited by clicking the Colors icon.

Select a color to edit. Change the color by either typing in new RGB values or drag the cursor around the color space by holding the mouse button down. Release the button when you find the correct color. The "Save as default colors" checkbox will save the selected colors for all titles that use subtitles, not just the current one

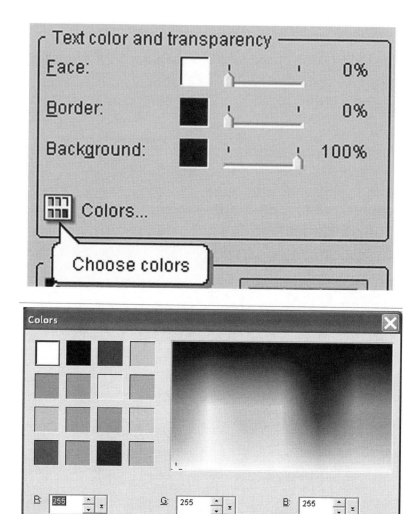

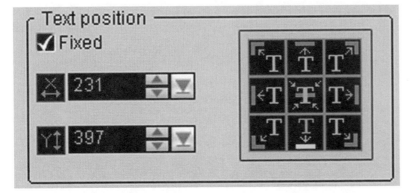

Positioning Subtitles on the Screen

Subtitles may be positioned automatically to any of the nine positions indicated in the diagram in the Text Position Control Panel or manually by unchecking the Fixed checkbox. Manual positioning may be accomplished by entering X and Y coordinates or by dragging the text box in the Preview window.

Previewing Subtitles in the Edit Screen Preview Window

Subtitle tracks may be previewed in the Preview window of the Edit screen. Select a subtitle track to preview by clicking the "Switch to another audio and/or subtitle track" icon at the bottom right of the Preview window and select the appropriate subtitle track to view.

Working with AC-3 5.1 Audio Files (Dolby Digital Audio)

If importing 5.1 AC-3 files as replacement audio tracks, be certain that Convert to Disc Template is not selected or the audio file will be recompressed as a stereo file.

DVD Workshop cannot create surround/5.1 audio files, nor can it encode 5.1 PCM files to AC-3 formatting. However, applications such as Adobe's Audition, Sony's Vegas, and other multitrack audio tools are capable of creating 5.1 audio files that may be used in DVD Workshop.

AC-3 5.1 audio files (also called Dolby Digital) may be imported into the Library and inserted into an audio track in the same manner as any other audio file. DVD Workshop will allow AC-3 5.1 audio files to pass through the Finish step without being re-rendered if Convert to Disc Template is not selected. The six channels (left, right, center, surround-left, surround-right, and sub) will be preserved in the final project.

If Convert to Disc Template is selected, then the AC-3 5.1 will be converted to a two-track (stereo) audio format since that is the only format that DVD Workshop can encode for AC-3 audio. Do not re-encode AC-3 audio files if you want to retain the 5.1 channels of the audio stream.

Although the audio properties panel doesn't display the number of tracks in an AC-3 audio stream, you can generally distinguish a two-track AC-3 file from a 5.1 AC-3 file by the bitrate. 5.1 AC-3 files are 448kbps, but two-track AC-3 files are usually encoded at much lower bitrates such as 192kbps.

```
┌─Audio────────────────────────────────────────────────┐
│                                                        │
│      Audio type:    Dolby Digital Audio                │
│   Total samples:    5,604,864 Samples                  │
│      Attributes:    48000 Hz                           │
│           Layer:                                       │
│        Bit rate:    448 kbps                           │
│                                                        │
└────────────────────────────────────────────────────────┘
```

Chapter 5

Finish Authoring

The final step in the DVD authoring process consists of checking the operation of your project and outputting it in your format of choice.

This may be a single layer DVD-5 disc, a dual layer DVD-9 disc, or a digital linear tape (DLT). In addition, Macrovision copy protection, CSS encryption, region codes, and an extra data folder may be added to your final burned DVD.

Previewing a Project

Although you may preview titles in the Edit Preview window or menus in the Menu Preview window, only the Finish Preview window allows you to immediately check all of the titles, menus, buttons, and other features in your completed project. The aspect ratio is always set to 16:9 whether the files are 4:3 or 16:9. This will not stretch 4:3 video to the 16:9 aspect ratio, it merely displays the video as 4:3 within the widescreen display.

Navigating with the Remote Control

The remote control in the Finish screen simulates the functions of the remote control for a set-top or software DVD player. Click the Play button or press the spacebar to start your project playing. The first-play video (if the project includes one) or the first menu will begin to play. Click the Stop button or press S to stop playback.

The left portion of the remote control displays the title (for DVDs), chapter, time, audio track, and subtitle track information. In this example, Chapter 2 of Title 2 (its position in the Title List) is 12 seconds into play. Audio Track 1 (of 3) is selected and subtitles are off.

Navigation from button to button within a menu may be accomplished with either the mouse or the direction buttons (DVD only), which are arranged in a circle. Click the center direction button or press Enter to activate a menu item. The arrow keys may also be used to navigate around a menu.

The buttons that look like fast-forward and rewind controls are used to move forward and backward through menus in the Menu List. You can also press the Page Up key to move forward and Page Down key to move backward.

Clicking the "Go to title menu" button or pressing the T key will bring up the menu that was last displayed. Clicking the next icon, the "Go to root menu" icon, or pressing the M key will play the first menu in the Menu List. Menu selection is available only in DVD projects.

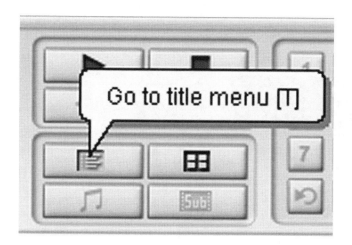

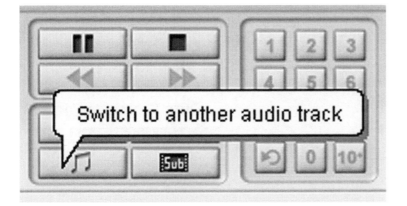

If the currently playing title has more than one audio track, you may switch tracks by clicking the button with the musical notes on it. The button to its right, labeled "Sub," is used to turn on and select subtitle tracks. Both functions apply only to DVD projects.

The keypad is used in VCD and SVCD projects to select titles to play. The Return button, at the lower-left portion of the keypad, plays the previous menu page

Working with Disc Templates

Although the use of disc templates was covered in Chapter 1, disc templates are typically fine-tuned during the Finish step of authoring.

In order to access the disc templates dialog from the Finish step, click the Burn Project to Disc icon.

Select the Disc Template Manager from the Burn Project to Disc dialog to access disc template settings from the Finish screen.

Required/Available hard drive space: 1.4 GB / 14.1 GB

Required/Available disc space: 890.2 MB / 4.4 GB

Burning progress: Elapsed time:

0%

Erase Disc   Burn   Close

Make Disc Options

Ulead DVD Workshop | General | Compression

Media type: NTSC DVD

70

Speed   Quality

Video settings

I-frames only

Video data rate: Variable   5000   kbps

Audio settings

Audio format: Dolby Digital audio

Audio type: 2/0(L,R)

Audio frequency: 48000   Hz

Audio bit rate: 192   kbps

OK   Cancel

Optimizing Disc Template Settings

If your project doesn't use any compliant media (all titles will be converted), then select the highest video bitrate that will fit the project onto a disc in order to maximize video quality. As for audio, an AC3 audio setting of 192kbps yields a very high-quality audio track without using a lot of bandwidth. At the bottom of the Burn Project to Disc dialog there is "Required/Available disc space" information. Gradually lower the MPEG encoding bitrate while checking the project size until the project fits on the disc.

If your project contains a mix of compliant and non-compliant video media you may need to select Convert to Disc for some of the titles that were encoded at video bitrates higher than the current project setting to fit the project onto the disc. Gradually lower the project encoding bitrate and/or convert additional compliant titles until the project fits on the disc.

It's not recommended to reduce the video bitrate to below about 5000kbps, or video quality may begin to noticeably suffer. One symptom of using too low a bitrate is macroblocking, or visible blocks in the image during high-motion scenes. Test different encoding bitrates by creating DVD project folders (see the Burning to Disc section) before committing a project to disc!

Remember to set the Speed/Quality slider set to 100 percent quality for the best (and slowest) video encoding quality.

Project Details Check

Overlapping button(s) found in:
        Menu name: < MENU-02 >

Lost menu link(s) found in:
        Menu name: < MENU-08 >
        Menu name: < MENU-05 >
        Menu name: < MENU-01 >
        Menu name: < MENU-09 >
        Menu name: < MENU-10 >
        Menu name: < MENU-11 >

Lost title link(s) found in:
        Title name: < Video Title 2 >

Continue   Close

Error Message Entering the Finish Step

DVD Workshop will perform a Project Details Check upon entering the Finish screen, checking for lost links and overlapping buttons.

Overlapping Buttons

In order to quickly identify overlapping buttons, enable Show/Hide Object Boundary (Alt+O) in the Menu screen, and select the menu(s) indicated in the Project Details Check dialog to have overlapping buttons.

Show/Hide Object Boundary [Alt+O]

Adjust the buttons so that they do not overlap.

Lost Menu and Title Links

If a menu doesn't have any linked buttons on it or if media is moved around so that links become unavailable, then DVD Workshop will designate this menu as having lost links. Identify the buttons with lost links by checking the link information in the Playlist panel in the Menu screen. Titles with lost associated media are easy to spot in the Title List since their thumbnails are video test patterns.

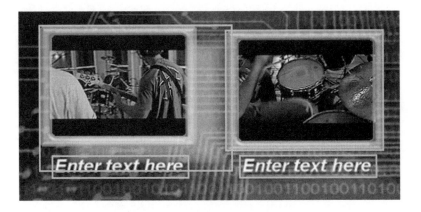

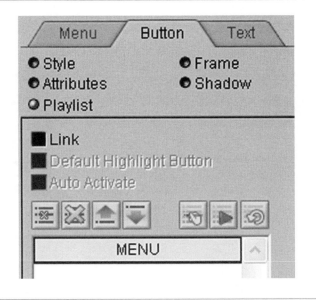

Objects Outside of the Safe Titling
Area

Although DVD Workshop will not
warn you of this, make sure all of the
objects that you want visible on the
screen are inside of the Safe Titling

Area.

Burning to Disc Options

Click the Burn Project to Disc icon
in the Remote Control in the Finish
screen. Before burning a disc there are
a number of settings in this dialog that
need to be checked or set.

By selecting the appropriate checkbox in the Output Settings area you may burn a project to disc, create DVD folders, and/or create a disc image (*.iso) of the project.

Burning a Project to Disc

Select a disc template and a working directory from the Burn tab of the Burn Project to Disc dialog. This is where DVD Workshop stores temporary files while it renders and burns the project.

Check to make sure there is sufficient hard drive space and disc space for the project before beginning to record. These items are located at the bottom of the Burn tab in the Burn Project to Disc dialog.

Click the "Burn to disc" checkbox and type in a project name.

Required/Available hard drive space:	393.4 MB / 13.6 GB
Required/Available disc space:	375.6 MB / 4.4 GB
Burning progress:	Elapsed time:

The project name will be the name that appears in the root directory of the burned disc. In this example the project name is "Project 3."

Disc Burner Settings

Select the DVD recorder you would like to use if you have more than one installed on your system, the speed at which you would like to record the disc, and the number of discs you will be making. Remember to only record the dick at the maximum speed of the media you are using. If you are getting errors on the final disc try recording at a lower speed.

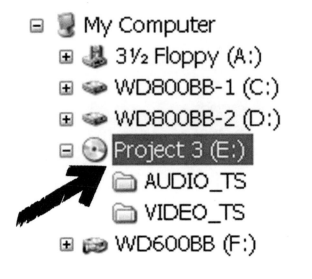

Advanced Settings for DVD +R/-R/CDR

There are several options in the Advanced Settings tab. Clicking "Perform write test before burning" will make sure your computer is fast enough to burn a disc. Select "Buffer underrun protection" if available because it will help to prevent writing errors due to your system not being able to keep up with the writing process. Selecting "Do not close disc" will allow further information to be written to the disc later.

Burner Advanced Settings for DVD +RW/-RW

"Quick eject" and Format DVD+RW" apply only to DVD+RW discs. Although formatting DVD+RW discs will make the burn stage take longer, it is strongly recommended. Selecting "Do not close disc" (DVD–RW only) will allow further information to be written to the disc later.

Can I Include Additional Files with My Project?

You can do this in Burn Project to Disc>Advanced Settings tab. Selecting "Include extra folder to disc" allows you to include additional files with the project assuming that there is sufficient disc space available. Click the "..." icon to browse to the folder you would like to include.

The extra folder will be placed in the root directory of the disc. In this example the folder "101CANON" has been included with the DVD project folders

Use the Extra Folder to Disc feature to include executable files such as applications, image files such as photos, Excel files, MIDI files, or any other file formats that should be distributed with the DVD. This is an excellent feature for a training disc that might include additional media for training use.

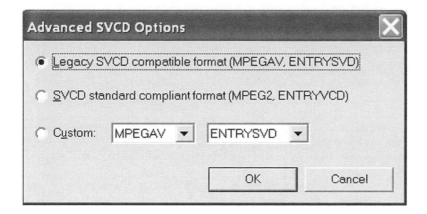

Advanced SVCD Options

The Advanced SVCD Options dialog allows for the selection of standard, legacy, or custom SVCD output formats. Standard is recommended but you may want to try legacy or a custom setting if your disc doesn't play.

What Is Macrovision?

Macrovision® is an analog copy-protection measure that scrambles the analog output of a video signal so that analog copying is not possible. If you plan to replicate your disc using a major manufacturing facility you will need an agreement with Macrovision. Navigate to Burn Project to Disc>Advanced Settings tab to access this feature.

Using Macrovision will incur a small charge from your DVD replication service as part of their license. Some replicators will require you to make arrangements with Macrovision directly.

What Are Region Codes?

Most set-top DVD players are set to play only DVD discs encoded with the region code where they were sold. Unless you would like to limit the players your disc will be able to be viewed on, leave all regions selected.

Adding Converted Files to the Library

If you want to add converted files to the Library, select this option. Any audio and video files that are converted to the disc template will be added to the Library. This feature is located on the Burn Project to Disc>Advanced Settings tab.

It is also possible to select the Library folder to which you want to add the converted file by clicking the "..." button next to the option dialog. Select or create the Library folder you would like to use.

Burning the Disc

After you have checked all of the settings, click "Burn" to begin recording the disc. DVD Workshop will describe each action as the disc-creation operation proceeds.

Creating DVD Folders?

DVD folders can be used to test the functions of the project using a software DVD player. This is a more rigorous compatibility test than the Preview screen's Remote Control. In addition, the DVD folders can be used to burn a project to disc. The DVD folders will be created in the working directory. Navigate to Burn Project to Disc>Burn tab to access this feature.

Previewing a Project from the DVD Folders

If you have a software DVD player that will play VOB files you may check the functionality of the project from the DVD folders. Direct your software DVD player to the VIDEO_TS.IFO file to play the project, or double-click this file to begin play.

Creating a Disc Image File (*.iso)

A disc image (*.iso) is a single file that contains all of the information for the project. Navigate to Burn Project to Disc>Burn tab to access this feature.

The disc image file will be created in the working directory and will have the volume name in the "Output settings" pane of the Burn Project to Disc>Burn tab.

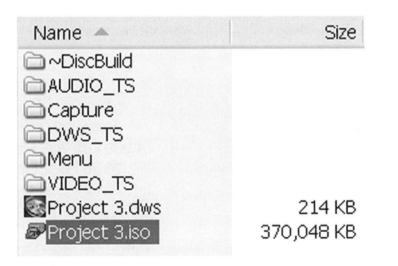

Burning a Disc from a Disc Image or DVD Folders

Burning from a disc image or DVD folders is the fastest way to burn a disc because rendering and encoding of the project is not necessary; these files already contain an image of the completed project. Click the ISO button on the Remote Control in the Finish screen to open the Burn from Disc Image or DVD Folder dialog.

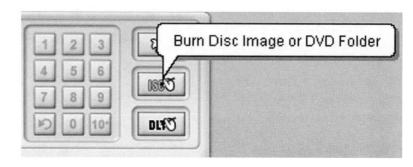

Select "Disc image" if you will be burning from a *.iso file or "DVD folder" if you will be burning from disc folders. If you are burning from DVD folders you may type in a volume name. The volume name for a disc image defaults to the disc image filename.

Click the "..." button to the right of the disc image path and browse to the disc image or DVD folder and click OK. The rest of the options on this page have been explained in the previous section. Click Burn to begin burning the disc.

Why Output to Digital Linear Tape? (DLT)

DLT is the industry-standard master-tape format for mass replication. In addition, the DLT output option can accommodate the DVD-9 (dual layer) disc specification for projects longer than 4.4GB (DVD-5 discs).

The Ulead DLT Writer dialog contains all of the information to be written to the tape and to be included in the finished DVDs. A disc image must be used when writing to DLT. Select a disc image by clicking the "..." button at the top of this dialog.

DDPID Information

The Disc Description Protocol ID information describes how your project will be mastered. The current "DVD part version" is 1.0. Select the type of disc you will be recording on in the "DVD book version" field. Choose "Read-only disc" for DVD-ROMs, "Rewritable disc" for DVD+RW/-RW/-RAM discs, and "Recordable" for DVD +R/-R discs.

The "Track path" pop-up menu applies only to dual-layer (DVD-9) discs. This setting refers to how the layers of the disc are read by the laser of the DVD player, in the same direction or opposite directions. "Parallel" is generally used for DVD-ROMs where fast access time is important or movies where a variation of the movie is on the second layer. For a single length movie the "Opposite" setting is recommended so that the layer change occurs as fast as possible.

This dialog sets the minimum readout rate of the final disc in Mbps (millions of bits per second).

Track path: Opposite ▼
Parallel
Opposite

Minimum readout rate: 5.04 Mbps ▼
2.52 Mbps
5.04 Mbps
10.08 Mbps

What Is CSS?

Content Scrambling System (CSS) is
a digital copy-protection system that
prevents DVD folders from being
copied directly to a hard drive or being
played back on a player without the
proper decoder. Commercial DVDs use
CSS. Select the regions in which you
would like the disc to be playable.

CSS options and region code
☑ Apply CSS   ☑ Region code
☑ 1 ☑ 2 ☑ 3 ☑ 4
☑ 5 ☑ 6 ☑ 7 ☑ 8

DVD-9 Options

If you would like to create DVD-9 discs,
check the Use DVD-9 checkbox. Selecting "Align split point to cell boundary"
will instruct DVD Workshop to set a
layer transition point (split point) that
provides the smoothest transition.
Alternately you may manually select
a split point. Remember that the first
layer should be equal to or larger in
size than the first layer.

DVD-9
☑ Use DVD-9   ☐ Align split point to cell boundary
Split point between layer for DVD-9 (x16 sectors):   5783

Output Options

Select the working directory for the DLT writer. This is where all DLT files will be stored. It's recommended to select "Verify after writing." This option will crosscheck the DLT file with the disc image file from which it was created. The rest of the options in the dialog should be set after conferring with your replicating house.

Writing to Digital Linear Tape

After double-checking all settings with your replicating house, click Write to begin writing to the DLT.

Coping with Playback Issues and Common DVD Mistakes

Pixilated Images and Optimizing MPEG Compression

Scenes with high motion, fire, or water waves are especially difficult to encode because of the random nature of the movement. It's difficult for the codec to predict what the next frame will look like.

The difference between 2000kbps and 6000kbps encoding for this water scene is more dramatic than the frame captures suggest. The 6000kpbs video is of good quality, while the 2000kpbs clip is badly pixilated.

The 8000kbps clip shows negligible improvement over the 6000kbps clip. Encode your video clips at a few different bitrates to find the sweet spot so that you don't waste disc space. Each clip may need to be encoded at a different bitrate depending on the content to achieve the best results.

Video That Stutters with Horizontal Motion

Video that stutters or jumps when there is horizontal motion is usually caused by incorrect frame order. Instead of playing the fields 1a-1b-2a-2b they are played 1b-1a-2b-2a, causing a large jump in motion from frame 1a to frame 2b. You may need to recapture the clip using a different frame order from the Capture screen>Capture Options>Change Frame Order dialog.

Change Field Order ✕

Field order: Upper Field First ▼
                Lower Field First
                Upper Field First

Processing...   0 %

[Detect]   [OK]   [Cancel]

Out of Disk Space Error

If while creating a disc image file (*.iso) you receive an "Out of Disk Space" message, even though you have plenty of room on your hard drive, it's possible you're running into a FAT32 limitation. You can check the file system of your computer by clicking on the C: drive and selecting Properties. Use NTFS to avoid this issue.

Chapter 6

Makin' It Great!

The technical and creative tips in this chapter might turn a good DVD layout into a great one. The menu links and appearance are a big part of what makes a DVD interesting ... or not. Try some of these workflows and see what a difference it makes in your project.

Authoring Tips

1. Sketch the layout for your project before you start authoring.
2. Try to match menu design with title content.
3. Keep first play videos brief.
4. Minimize unnecessary menu objects.
5. Choose chapter points to create smooth menu to title transitions.
6. Use an NLE to edit video and audio.
7. Keep color channel values within legal values.
8. Avoid fancy hard to read fonts.
9. Keep font size 14 point or larger.
10. Preprocess video in an NLE to increase compression efficiency.
11. Keep DVD Workshop 2.0's compositing ability in mind while authoring.
12. Remember that you can import objects created in Cool 3D Studio and PhotoImpact XL in DVD Workshop 2.0.

Menu Navigation and Planning a Disc Project

Just like your teacher used to tell you, "Plan your work and work your plan."

As was mentioned in Chapter 2, it's a good idea to sketch out the linking behavior of the menus in your project before you start to create it. Using pencil and paper is a good idea, just to map out the disc.

It should be very obvious to the viewer how to navigate your DVD. If the menus are too complicated, or if it isn't obvious what content is contained in each menu, then the frustrated viewer may lose interest in the DVD before even viewing it! Keep it clear.

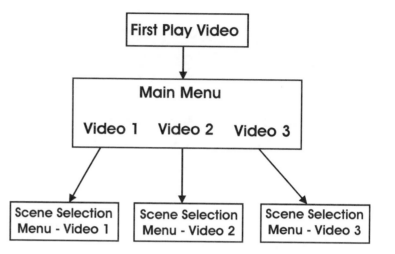

Try to relate the design of the menus with the content of the disc. A good menu will use elements of the media contained on the disc to give the disc a cohesive feel. In this example a motion menu was created by panning on a still life of the wedding program and flowers.

Remember that the viewer will have to sit through the introductory video every time the disc is played. As a general rule keep introductory videos to 10 or 15 seconds. Unless there is a reason for an introductory video, get to that first menu as fast as possible.

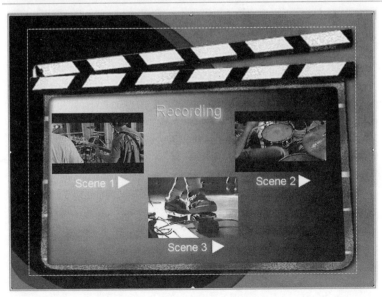

Sometime a good DVD menu can be turned into a great DVD menu by removing unnecessary items. What's not there can be just as important as what is there. B.B. King once said, "It's not the notes I play but the silence in between that counts." In a menu, sometimes less is more.

Study the menus of commercially produced DVDs or DVDs your friends have created. Take mental notes regarding which design elements enhance the content of the DVD and which do not. In this WWII documentary the motion background consists of major battle names scrolling down the screen to get the viewer in the mood of what is to come.

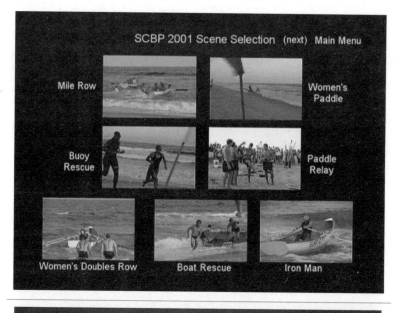

Easter Eggs (Invisible Buttons)

It has been commonplace for commercial DVDs to include easter eggs, or buttons that are invisible. These are powerful and fun when used creatively.

These buttons appear when in the highlight or rollover state. The titles linked to these easter eggs are usually outtakes or other "making of" video.

To make an object button invisible, first select the button to be made invisible. Select the Invisible Button option from the Menu screen>Button tab>Style Option panel. The button will be visible only when in the rollover state.

To make a text button invisible, first select the text to be made invisible. Select the Invisible Button option from the Menu screen>Text tab>Style Option panel. The text button will be visible only when in the rollover state.

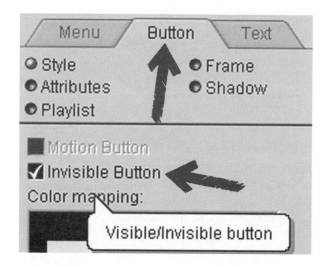

Visible/Invisible button

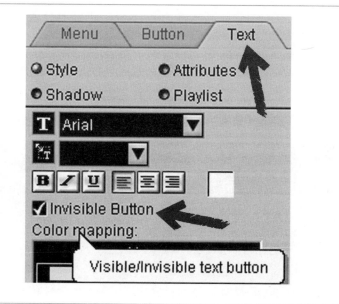

Visible/Invisible text button

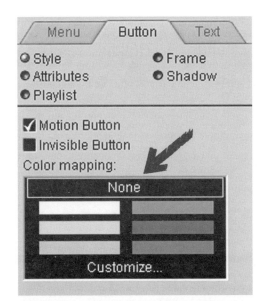

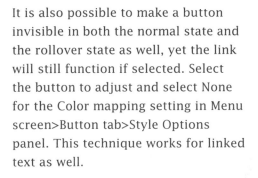

It is also possible to make a button invisible in both the normal state and the rollover state as well, yet the link will still function if selected. Select the button to adjust and select None for the Color mapping setting in Menu screen>Button tab>Style Options panel. This technique works for linked text as well.

You can view the location of invisible buttons by selecting Show/Hide Object Boundaries (Alt+O) at the bottom right of the Menu Preview window.

Editing for Seamless Menu to Title Transitions

Try to break video clips into scenes while editing in the NLE (nonlinear editor). A good method is to fade to black and from black in between each important scene in the video. Set the black portions of the video (between scenes) as chapter points in DVD Workshop to create smooth video transitions from menus to titles.

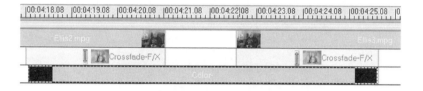

Remember to fade-in and fade-out the audio as the video fades to and from black at the end of each scene. Although audio fade-in and fade-out can be done in DVD Workshop, better control is available in the NLE.

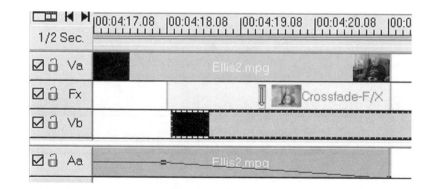

If you aren't going to be editing your title in an NLE, pick chapter points based on the content of the video clip. A change of environment (indoors to outdoors or vice-versa), or change of activities are examples of good chapter point locations.

Remember to select I-frames from the Edit>Video Control Panel when selecting chapter points to avoid corrupting frames.

☑ Locate I-frame

⬛ Convert to Disc Template

Select to search only for I-frames in the clip

Keeping Colors Legal and Text Readable

RGB color channel values between 16 and 235 are considered legal colors. Illegal colors bloom and buzz on the video display and can even have a negative effect on the audio contained in the project. See the Glossary for more information on illegal colors.

Whites should have a maximum brightness of 50 percent, less if they are on a black or very dark background. Also reduce the saturation of colors, and remember to check colors on a TV screen, because computer monitors are usually more subdued than TVs.

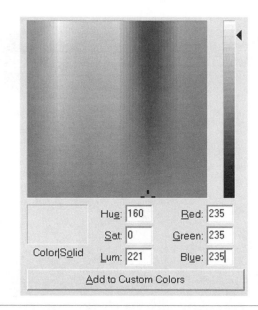

Keep Font Size 14 Point or Larger

Lucida Sans Unicode 8

Lucida Sans Unicode 10

Lucida Sans Unicode 12

Lucida Sans Unicode 14

Lucida Sans Unicode 16

Keep in mind that computer monitors operate at a much higher resolution than TVs. Font sizes should be 14 points or larger. You may be able to get away with a 12-point font depending on the font style and background and font color if you're really squeezed for space.

Avoid fonts with serifs or other fancy curves. The smaller the font size, the more critical it is to stay with a simple font. Some of the fancier fonts may work at larger sizes. Outlines colors that are in between the font and background color can help the text or object to pop off of the background.

Good Font Choices

Arial
AvantGarde Bk BT
Lucida Sans Unicode
Verdana
Tahoma

Bad Font Choices

Blackletter686 BT
Rauch LET
ParkAvenue BT
Tiranti Solid LET

Preprocessing Video in the NLE for Best Results

Contrast, or applying a little noise reduction or blurring of the video can also reduce noise. Because noise is random in nature, it consumes a lot of bandwidth that could be better used for the actual image.

Since it's easy to go overboard with these settings, make sure you perform a few tests to be sure you're improving the final result.

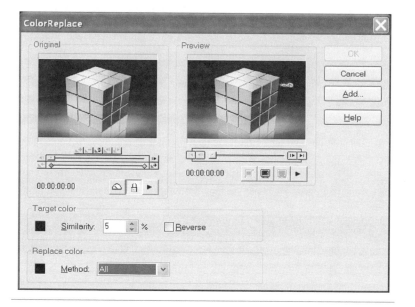

Since there are many levels of black that are not perceived in the image on a TV, another bandwidth-conserving tip for MPEG compression is to compress the range of blacks in a video. Most NLEs have a plug-in or filter to accomplish this. The plug-in shown will replace a color with a range of ones close to it. This is known as crushing the blacks.

Analog capture will show a corrupt area around the perimeter of the image known as fringing. This random pattern also consumes a lot of compression bandwidth. Crop out the fringing using a NLE. Digital video also exhibits this fringing, although to a lesser degree, because of variances in the voltage across the CCD sensor (charge coupled device).

Try to limit zooming and panning, or edit the video before compression to reduce or eliminate zooming and panning. Not only are these techniques indicative of amateur video, but they also consume a large amount of disk space. In addition, unless you shoot with great lighting, you will most likely end up with blurred images.

DV cameras have a different type of fringing, found on the left and right edges of the screen. Crop this as well. Some cameras leave six pixels on both sides of the video as black. Crop these out if your camera leaves the black edge.

A good lighting package will make a tremendous difference in the quality of your video production. Lighting for DV is very important whether it's simply a reflector or a full on kit. We recommend taking a look at http://www/ photoflex.com and seeing their online university for lighting techniques and training.

Reducing color saturation, sometimes as much as 15 percent in your NLE, can make a tremendous difference to how the encoder and compressor will work. High-motion scenes may need to have even more color reduced in order to produce the best picture. This is done in the editing process with your non-linear editor. Video captured directly to DVD Workshop cannot have color processing done to it unless it is opened in an NLE of some sort.

Another great method of getting a good encode to MPEG is to use hardware. ADS technologies (http://www.adstech.com) has a product called an AV Link. This device can convert to MPEG on the fly and will remove the heavy encoding load from your CPU while providing a very high-quality encode, typically better in quality than a software encode. DVD Workshop will recognize the MPEG video stream coming in over the FireWire port and capture the video in real time. The video can then be edited in Media Studio Pro or another NLE for use in DVD Workshop.

If you have a slower computer, one recommendation is to print your video

Video "Intr_NTSC" used as a motion video in the background. Image "BG57" imported as an object with 50% transparency and then sized to fit the preview window.

to DV, then output the DV stream from the deck/camera to the DV Link, encoding in real-time, and capturing the MPEG stream with DVD Workshop. Then the MPEG video can be prepared for a menu just like any other video.

Another great technique is to composite one motion image on top of a still or video image as a background. By dropping an image as a button on the screen and stretching it to a new size, either in aspect or not, and reducing its transparency to 50 percent or less, it's easy to make a static or less-exciting image appear to have a lot going on.

If you have Ulead's Cool 3D production package, you can also use 3D overlays as buttons in DVD Workshop. DVD Workshop will automatically read the alpha channel contained in a 32-bit AVI file exported from Cool 3D or other 3D animation applications. Nothing needs to be done. Just import the 3D button to your library like you would with any other video or image and use it as a button or overlay.

VASST is Video, Audio, Surround, and Streaming Training. Here at VASST we help you master your preferred topic faster than you ever expected with immediate, accessible and thorough information. We offer a variety of training materials for different learning styles.

Whether you are looking for a book, a DVD, or an on-site trainer, VASST can provide tips, techniques, and solutions for all your media needs.

VASST Training Tours: visit vasst.com for current tour dates. We offer seminars on Cameras, Lighting, Editing, Surround Sound, and other general media topics. Training on specific applications by companies such as Adobe, Sony, Ulead, Pinnacle, AVID, Boris, and Apple is also available.

www.vasst.com

Instant Sound Forge

Jeffrey P. Fisher

Get working with Sony's Sound Forge software in an instant. This accessible and thorough orientation features detailed screen shots and step-by-step directions. You learn the full range of functions as well as professional techniques for polish and efficient workflow.

$24.95, Softcover, 208 pp, ISBN 1-57820-244-2 **Available July, 2004**

After Effects On the Spot

Richard Harrington, Rachel Max, & Marcus Geduld

Packed with more than 400 expert techniques, this book clearly illustrates the essential methods that pros use to get the job done with After Effects. Experienced motion graphic artists and novices alike discover an invaluable reference filled with ways to improve efficiency and creativity.

$27.95, Softcover, 288 pp, ISBN 1-57820-239-6

Instant Vegas 5

Douglas Spotted Eagle

Get working with Sony's Vegas 5 software in an instant. This accessible and thorough orientation features detailed screen shots and step-by-step directions. You learn the full range of functions as well as professional techniques for polish and efficient workflow.

$24.95, Softcover, 208 pp, ISBN 1-57820-260-4 **Available August, 2004**

CMP**Books**